The Changing Guise of Myths

Modernity in Question
Studies in Philosophy, Sociology and History of Ideas

Edited by Małgorzata Kowalska

Volume 1

PL ACADEMIC RESEARCH

Andrzej Leder

The Changing Guise
of Myths
Philosophical Essays

Translated by Richard Reisner

PL ACADEMIC RESEARCH

Bibliographic Information published by the Deutsche Nationalbibliothek
The Deutsche Nationalbibliothek lists this publication in the Deutsche
Nationalbibliografie; detailed bibliographic data is available in the internet
at http://dnb.d-nb.de.

The publication was financially supported by the Ministry of Science
and Higher Education National Programme for the Development of Humanities

NARODOWY PROGRAM
ROZWOJU HUMANISTYKI

Cover image: © Justyna Kowalska-Leder

Library of Congress Cataloging-in-Publication Data

Leder, Andrzej.
    The changing guise of myths : philosophical essays / Andrzej Leder. — Edition 1.
        pages cm. — (Modernity in question. Studies in philosophy, sociology and history
of ideas, ISSN 2193-3421 ; volume 1)
    ISBN 978-3-631-63225-3 (print) — ISBN 978-3-653-03596-4 (e-Book)
    1. Europe, Eastern—History—1989- 2. Myth—Social aspects—Europe, Eastern. 3.
Post-communism—Social aspects—Europe, Eastern. 4. Capitalism—Europe, Eastern. 5.
Social change—Europe, Eastern. 6. Self-perception—Europe, Eastern. I. Title.
    DJK51.L435 2013
    947.0009'051—dc23

2013030184

ISSN 2193-3421
ISBN 978-3-631-63225-3 (Print)
E-ISBN 978-3-653-03596-4 (E-Book)
DOI 10.3726/978-3-653-03596-4

© Peter Lang GmbH
Internationaler Verlag der Wissenschaften
Frankfurt am Main 2013
All rights reserved.
PL Academic Research is an Imprint of Peter Lang GmbH.

Peter Lang – Frankfurt am Main · Bern · Bruxelles · New York ·
Oxford · Warszawa · Wien

www.peterlang.de

Table of contents

1. The question of longevity...

The changing guise of myths

When Christopher Columbus set foot on a beach in the Antilles, the Middle Ages had come to a close. For the Spanish soldiers, sailors and *hidalgos* though, modern forms of plunder and conversion of the native Indians did not surely differ in any particular way from that practiced in the Middle Ages in respect to the Moors from Granada. This was still the same world of Christians and Pagans, soldier-faith and service to the Devil – a world whose meaning God himself guaranteed, in return demanding 'no surrender' and cruelty. After all, as if to calm the non-believers, both Moors and Indians were of brown skin.

Each of us, waking in the morning, has to open the world we have woken into. In fact, we have to create it anew. We have to endow meaning to people, objects and tasks – have to secure a place in the chaos of time passing. When opening their eyes during the palpable reality of a dream, a person will dream beyond the dream, will carry over meanings and experiences from one sphere to another, and the whistle of the kettle just a moment before, will read as the signal of a departing train.

The sound of water boiling, song of birds outside the window, voice coming from a radio – are signs that reality exists, thanks to which it is possible to open the world. The experience of people locked up in isolation cells and deprived of experiencing the senses is well known. Not much is required for the world to simply go and out of the emptiness, for hallucinations to begin to emerge.

The rustle of leaves carried by the wind, the coarseness of bed sheets, growl of cars coming from the street, stain on a wall, newspaper by the bed, someone's breath just behind you, the smell of coffee, someone cursing next door, the feeling of hunger and queasiness... How then to join these 'signs' into a cohesive whole that comes to make up my own world, the space whose opposite ends delineate my movements? A source of meaning thus is required, transforming the simplest desires in the entire gamut of the world we know. A myth is necessary. One that "crams people's experience into a certain whole, (...) gives direction and meaning. One that together with recollection and expectation (...), creates an understanding of human reality"[1] – as Paul Ricoeur finely put it. Without this the passing stream of 'signs' is incomprehensible, without this there is no world.

In the mid 1980s, in Poland, an East European country under Soviet Domination, Mr. P. about whom there will be more later, woke as usual early in the morning and listened to a certain radio programme. Neither the news nor music was of interest to him. He didn't believe the news and the music selected by the DJ was not to his liking. Most important though was the tenor of the speaker's voice. This voice, in fact, allowed him to remember his own myth and give meaning to the hours ahead – an ironic, sarcastic tone, as if saying to Mr. P. 'My God, how absurd our world is, we're surrounded by nonsense, stupidity and evil! But despite this we in fact exist! We're sad, bitter, in the dumps, but we exist! Our life therefore has a life of its own, independent of this stupidity, evil and absurdity'. And then Mr. P. sensed that he in fact, exists. 'I am', he sensed. 'Against the odds – I exist.' And this was paradoxically a triumph. This was a triumph on the part of the speaker, Mr. P. and all of us, a triumph over the empty, nonsensical existence. Mr. P. would go to his Institute, to his 'research' and found others that also existed, against the odds.

In essence this was probably about the primeval myth of the dragon embodying chaos and the battle with it, a battle in which existence is created. The absurdity of that existence was a monster with which Mr. P. would struggle. Thanks to the presence of that dragon, he in the process became a St. George figure. But at that time, he still didn't understand that he would identify with St. George as long, and only as long, as the dragon existed, one that defied reason and its reality. After all, he never believed that the dragon could be slain. He simply domesticated it.

Since the time the country immersed itself in the world of global civilisation, Mr. P. wakes and hears that nappies, laptops and warehouses of Spanish terracotta exist in a way completely independent of him and in fact, he is defined now purely by all his consumer activities. And falls into despair. It is all so self-sufficient, sensible and purposeful that Mr. P's existence seems to be some sort of whim, an accidental addition devoid of all importance. The world has its own meaning and Mr. P. no longer needs to do the same 'meaning' every day, struggling with nonsense. If this were not enough – it is rather the world that defines the meaning of Mr. P.! Thus, the feeling of being shackled. Mr. P. is too sensible, or maybe too subtle, to claim that nappies and laptops also represent the dragon – he cannot be one of the 'outraged', an anarchist therefore,

---

1   Paul Ricoeur, *Finitude et Culpaibilite, t. II: La symbolique du mal*, Editions Aubier Montaigne, *Paris* 1976, p. 11, tr. Richard Reisner.

like his older son. Mr. P's dragon has simply dissolved. Now Mr. P. attempts in despair to reconstruct his myth, find the dragon that he can domesticate.

For Mrs. P. the dragon is the neighbour who buys a second car. Here though, not much has changed; in the previous communist system the neighbour built himself a summer cottage near Warsaw with materials sourced from 'impure' forces and still earlier issued (or not) passports to those wishing to travel. He was an apprentice to evil. Mrs. P. lives according to The Myth of The Wheel of Time and Eternal Return. The world is divided into opposite pairs: male-female, dark-light, pure-impure and above all, good-evil. Mrs. P. is on the side of good but this position sentences her to eternal frustration, for in the constant cycle of transformations there is no place for a definitive victory of good. The triumph of evil that returns, wearing other masks and sarcastically laughing in the face of the righteous, is for her just as certain as the fact that Mr. P. will never buy a second car.

That is why the short period of the Turning-Point filled her with anxiety when evil hid itself in a particularly cunning way. She tracked it down in her daughter, who after watching a television commercial unexpectedly demanded tampons and freedom. Mrs. P. quickly perceived the relationship between the new image of her child and the uncombed longhaired former Deputy Minister of Finance, who together with his superior destroyed her place of work. Evil took its place again and Mrs. P. shook her head and looking with despair at Mr. P. said: 'Well, you've got what you wanted'. For her, Mr. P. is the eternally deceived victim of the dragon who, with incomprehensible stubbornness, still shields himself before the truth.

Notwithstanding essential differences, before the Turning-Point, The Myth of the Dragon and The Myth of Eternal Return afforded both Mr. and Mrs. P. at least a mutual dollop of satisfaction in experiencing being helpless, evoked by their enveloping wasteland of reality. When, however, Polish society moved from the desert into the jungle full of temptations and dangers while the world around Mr. and Mrs. P. began to dramatically change, it transpired that the ability of these two mythological structures were two completely separate matters.

The myth of struggling with the dragon that is chaos, does not leave room for any positive changes whatsoever in reality. It assumes a balance of power. A change in this balance, victory for either side, removes the sense of the whole construction. Let us reiterate; Mr. P. was able to render meaning to the absurd only when that absurd in reality had no self-sufficient tempting image. All manner of temptation, everything that shines and at the same time is available, diverts Mr. P.'s attention from the effort of rendering chaos comprehensible through its negation – and propels him towards desires and the search for a role in what Mr. P. Junior calls the rat race. Mr. P. cannot resist his desire of goods that are new and tempting, sees that friends with whom he struggled in common with the monster are now living in the lap of luxury and demean him, paying for his restaurant meals. He is ill at ease because he no longer understands anything.

If it wasn't enough that his dragon has vanished, he is no longer the knight, herald of the Gods. Were he to accept the mythology of his son he would have to concede that he belongs to the rat species – or to begin wearing army boots and leather jacket like Mr. P. Junior. But that is not his mythology – Mr. P. knows full well that he would become pitiful, most of all to himself. For this, he is too honest. Nor does he wish to be a rat. Every morning out of fear and despair he attempts to discover himself anew, thinks about the day to come, reluctantly gets out of bed and at work where its superficiality is plain to see, a constant headache is his companion. He feels weak and at times, suspects that he has simply fallen ill.

The Myth of The Wheel of Time though, is much more resistant to changes in reality. This is an unusually archaic structure and therefore perhaps so enduring. Its endurance comes from its complete independence of the world out there. The fact itself of being a part of this world, independent from the will of Mrs. P. and thus not susceptible to her influence, means every event can become recognised as an example of evil. The more tempting the car is that Mr. P. never will buy, the more defined is the symbol of evil in action, an evil that simply hates Mrs. P. for her goodness, and this is why it sets about to tempt her.

Myth allows one to understand the world. Though this is not only about a certain verbal construction that can be read or told. Myth renders meaning to action – at every moment of every day. To understand the world means above all, to be able to live in this world. To live according to the meaning rendered to reality through myth – to continually play out the mythological play, to identify with a mythical character and to repeat those deeds that a myth gives authority to.

When evil has already been recognised, Mrs. P. is calm. She knows that the battle is not hers – it belongs to the 'hero'. She only has to maintain purity, hers and that of her kin – not to allow evil to take over their souls. Then she has to identify the 'hero', support him in his battle and – become betrayed when the 'hero' succumbs to temptation and goes over to the side of impure forces.

This is one of the motifs of the myth about waiting for the Messiah and false prophets assuming his identity. Because good itself, however, in this life cannot claim victory, Mrs. P. reconciles herself to her sad fate. And waits once more. She cannot bear though the fact that her daughter, ostentatiously ignores the eternal struggle in which Mrs. P. takes part, sells herself to all that is impure – treating the temptations of evil as something she is simply entitled to.

This in fact is what Mr. P. is most jealous of in his daughter. In the jungle of the contemporary being she has entered straight out of the myths of childhood, did not manage to consume the wasteland of the world that shaped her parents, did not even, as in the case of her older brother, become infected with rage. The bustling market that so tempts and at the same time repulses Mr. P. – both attracting and filling him with fear – is simply her market. When Mr. P. lately purchased grapes and brought them home, without telling anyone, she ate immediately half. Mr. P. reminded himself that back then when They, the communist authorities, 'presented' the Bulgarian grapes and sold them outside the 'peoples supermarket', suddenly a strange sense of community would appear. Those shopping were excited, the women argued, each carrying home their plunder would notice the fake smiles of jealousy. As a matter of rule, to make one's way across town with a bag of grapes – that was something! These are now but hallucinations. Compared to his daughter, with his present-day dragon and present fear of the unknown, Mr. P. feels as if he were back in the cave – with club and bearskin.

The constancy of the world for each of us is guaranteed by the compatibility of two totally different spheres – *the in* us and *the around* us. The mind and soul at work – *the in* us, is in itself not visible and in addition, works with those things that are not visible. Nonetheless it has to find them in *the around* us, in the world of palpable objects it identifies as signs of the not visible. The endurance of meanings is borne by myths, understood as a community, a community of myths. Its lack is emptiness and isolation.

Women, men and Plato

Thus two beings stand facing each other, who first are different and second, need, desperately need... As in Plato's myth, man is only one half searching for the other, from which he was torn apart. Incomplete, in need of completion.

This in fact is the concept chosen to write of women and men. After all, the very fact that one writes on humankind in terms of male and female, determines the pathways of thinking. We thus don't face the problem of humankind 'as a whole', before us a being defined by gender and forced to deal with all its consequences. This particular view also imposes understanding the relations between one person and another, between a man and a woman, where foremost lies the difference that determines human fate.

If myth speaks the truth, then the most important basis of life is re-unification – finding the other half and the [re]formation of a whole. Why is this so rarely a success? Why is the depressing sense of loneliness, incompletion, so commonplace among men and women? The dimension where the myth of two people meeting grows, has changed for good. How did this occur?

There are many dimensions that provide a possible means of making this narration possible. In its very self, however, in its assumptions that the most important is re-discovering oneself and the unification of two people, this myth situates itself in deep opposition against the spirit of civilisation in which we live. Our culture therefore places emphasis on the individual, on the otherness of every person. In our culture this otherness is protected – such is the understanding of freedom in whose name the Declaration of Human Rights has been written. This is a freedom 'from' – from violence, rape, from subjugation. In this regard it is a freedom from others, from all that is 'bad' in these others. In fact, to meet another person also signifies being close to their 'dark side', grievance and hatred, greed and brutal strength. In protecting us before all these, our culture protects us from the price necessary to pay for this closeness – and thus protects us also from closeness.

If we examine why such a price has to be paid for undergoing unity with another person, we shall be closer to answering why such a unity for us in our day and age is nearly impossible.

Plato's myth speaks of a mutual search. What does this metaphor signify? Those that search are those at a distance from one another. Distance can be understood physically as being lost in the crowd but distance, space, can also be marked out by difference. When someone searches for another – which is completely other, so other like a person of a different sex – they must complete a great and difficult journey. And for this, strength is required, one that allows for an odyssey across this void. Thus the issue of the relation between man and woman is always one of desire and strength. The striving for otherness. A strength that needs to be employed so that myth can find its completion.

This particular means of approaching the force, the culture in which we live, has set its first trap for us – Machiavelli being probably the first to discover this. He noticed a hidden trait that has to be paid for a 'Christian' reluctance to embrace such traits he named *virtu* – and most of all, to taking responsibility for violence.

All manner of violence and therefore also every functioning form of strength evokes fear. Fear of the one who has to take responsibility and the fear of those who are to be the subject of its function. Christianity seeks to protect us before this fear for it condemns force for its own sake – and the source of its strength places in transcendence. It protects weakness. Perhaps as Hobbes suspected, the religion of the hurt and subjugated was also the religion of the living in fear, those most of all desiring safety? More than justice, freedom or truth. Or closeness.

When therefore evil ceased to be seen in weakness, when thanks to Christianity people recognised that the responsibility of the strong is to give shelter to the weak, there occurred as Nietzsche wrote, an amazing 'reversal of values'. Thus when humility and weakness became a virtue, strength for its own sake and arbitrary, unjustified s t r i v i n g had – as a matter of course – to become a sin. He who dared to reach for these was guilty of the sin of pride and duly condemned. The problem being that closeness can only be attained thanks to an arbitrary, unjustified striving. Often known as love.

Let us repeat. In order for myth to be fulfilled, so that the respective halves could again become one, strength is required, an enormous strength. Though arising from a self-contained force, one that all too easily turns into violence, one a civilised person cannot make use of. For it is burdened with the stigma of guilt, for it evokes fear, for it renders powerless, for he who despite all reaches out for it, falls into sin and shall be cast out of human society. Striving for unification, he shall find himself in a void. And this is a trap which everyone encounters – whose desire is an enormous strength.

Two human beings – a woman and a man, face one another and attempt to resolve the problem of meeting and not paying the price for their desire.

When the right to reach for another person by means of primal force was questioned, it was necessary to find a means, which protecting the freedom of choice of all – regardless of their strength – allows two people to come together. Closeness was to be guaranteed by a gift, giving oneself completely by choice to another person. The knightly ideal of love, an ideal whose oldest record is in the verse of Provence poets – embodies this concept in splendid fashion. The swain offers himself to the damsel, offering her his longing and ample shoulders to rest upon. He does not expect anything from her – apart from agreement to serve. The damsel may accept his efforts and avail herself...

Let us take a careful look. Thus almost unnoticed, the authority to decide whether two people shall in fact meet or shall not meet, moves from the one who desires closeness – to the one who allows this desire. If the norm does not allow an intrusion into the space of the other, then closeness is determined by the person who is passive, the one who can – but doesn't have to – agree to this risk-laden adventure, which is the meeting. Regardless whether in fact this be a woman or a man.

Does expressing agreement for closeness though set free enough strength so that two human halves become one? Why would someone who has not the desire, not the strength arising from desire, complete the difficult journey separating them from the other? They are tempted therefore for this labour, to demand one way or another, a form of remuneration. Acceptance easily changes into a game of expectation: '...and what will I have in exchange?' – often the start of serving another purpose than desire, in fact the road to the market place.

This, however, means that a meeting is not possible. It would appear therefore that the only possible force capable of making sure that closeness occurs is in fact, the desire for closeness. If this is absent or too weak then closeness will not be achieved. Moreover, if a person attempts to allow for closeness in the name of something else – such as ambition, safety, pleasure or convenience – they may achieve what they are seeking, but certainly will not find the lost Platonic 'other half'. And they shall live alone, in separation.

Humans therefore are beings who can simulate closeness to themselves and others, though ones who can live without it, beings that can deceive themselves and others – die in spirit and live on, as if nothing had happened. And this is often their daily routine.

This is the new form of myth in which two halves come closer, are at each other's side but do not meet. Thus they remain, pretending to themselves and the world around them that they represent a whole. This is but a pretence, a lie for they are at a distance – maybe more than when they were at first separated. Then they knew of the missing, as if just after losing a hand and trying to use it, all the while experiencing a void. Now they have forgotten already and think that everything is as it should be. Loneliness is their fate.

Closeness, freedom, loneliness as well as the 'dimension of myth' are not objects that can be seen in the daily routine of reality that we are able to grasp. In the world that is readily available to us we have to deal only with their signs and symbols, or signifiers – such as words that are recorded, actions that they demand and finally, emotions that they evoke. These signs and symbols though have long since lost their singularity. Words and actions too often hide a void to be believed.

And our own affective journeys as a rule, we do not understand. Almost never do we pay much attention to such, though as – the now unfashionable – Sartre once wrote, in every such journey a person's whole existence is reflected and every emotion expresses this whole. Perhaps our existence has become too complex? Perhaps the continual interpretation of emotions is simply not possible for a human – at least because there is no time for this? How then is it possible to avoid becoming lost?

The bourgeois world has placed men and women in a fixed role that serves every gender. These roles have given a guarantee that in a paradoxical situation – when there is no force carrying people to one another other – each shall know what is expected, one from the other. As a consequence, however, something very dangerous has occurred. The disintegration of ties between true and deep relations between people and the formal construction of roles that regulate behaviour from day to day.

These two levels have ceased to relate to one another. It is only in this context that the role of pretence is understandable. In a changing world it is increasingly difficult to reduce to a simple ritual of matchmaking, weddings, christenings and funerals – unending varieties of forces and relationships arising between men and women. Pretence has allowed to join the unendingness of motives with a limited repertoire of behaviour. The roles played out, however, are increasingly less related to real people and increasingly mask their real nature, their strength and their aspirations.

Thus in the course of the last two centuries it has transpired that everyone can be anyone they wish and even that everyone has to be the one they can, where the formal construction of roles literally has collapsed like a house of cards. This has resulted in widespread confusion. A confusion in the sphere of expectations set to oneself, and others. A disorientation in the sphere of emotions, which expectations define as such, one affecting what role, what is being experienced now, relates to. And if Mr. P. were to define the state of spirit in which men and women most often make attempts at present towards building closeness, then he would call it in fact, disorientation.

This is not another tirade against emancipation, freedom of choice and individualism. Searching for one's place is a magnificent right given by our culture. Though an unforeseen effect of the breaking of ties that served to maintain at least an appearance of unity has become the placing of us all face to face with the above mentioned sense of confusion. Thus constantly defining anew the nature of relations that build closeness is costly, too costly...

This is the 20th century version of Plato's myth about beings searching for one another.

Version one. When *he* unites with *she* and desires her closeness so much that he loses his mind, her will no longer counts and is unable to bear the smallest of distances. *She* then becomes distant (from *he*), for *he* does not respect her freedom. Then *he* begins to wane in his heart, takes revenge, resorts to violence. And *she* wanes in her heart and betrays (*he*), so as to prove *she* is free.

Version two. When *she* desires closeness above all else, then out of fear of loss begins to watch (*he*), tie *he* in a thousand unseen lengths of thread until *he* feels stripped of freedom to the last centimetre and begins to struggle, resorts to drink and violence and *she* wanes in her heart, quietly fulfilling her role.

Version three. When the strivings of *he* have been quashed, when therefore dreaming of closeness *he* awaits a decision from *she* – and every explosion of resentment or spitefulness *he* treats as a change to that decision and is not ready to accept – *she* will disregard him, for the burden of carrying the whole falls on *she*. And *she* wanes in her heart and desperately seeks the one who would really have the strength to strive towards her, even in spite of *she* herself. And in *he* only bile is left.

Version four. When *she* herself recklessly searches for *he*, this begins to evoke fear and enmity. Though *she* does not resort to direct violence, the striving of *she* is rather too forceful. To those that *she* wishes to win over, her strength identifies with the loss of freedom – and departs too far from the role marked by her culture. *She* blunders from *rendez vous* to *rendez vous*, and subsequent partners quench their fear (of *she*) with a curt growl of 'hussy'.

There are many more possible versions. For example the one where striving has met its death in *she*, so she allows for a semblance of closeness, taking satisfaction only in one or another reward of make-believe. As well as...

The core of the Platonic myth is that their exist two separated, endlessly different halves that search for one another so as to form a lost whole.

The question of longevity...

Mr P. recently was sitting at the table with three friends. They were having a heated discussion and were heartily tucking into their supper. At one particular point he took leave of the discussion, looked at them – gesticulating with their arms and forks – and suddenly realised something, which sent a cold shiver down his spine. For each of his close friends already had one leg in the grave. And if not for the intervention of modern medicine they would simply be lying at the local cemetery by now – and not taking delight in the culinary delicacies only recently available.

Both women had haemorrhages, one during childbirth and the other as a result of an accident. His friend, for that matter, fell from the roof when overseas at work and for two weeks lay unconscious, breathing only with the aid of a machine that was essential to do the work for him. Mr. P. was sitting at the table with three ghosts – and suddenly felt alone. Fortunately, only for a moment.

He would no doubt have felt alone all the time had he lived a century before. He would be a widower by now who had been to the funerals of two friends – looking at the world afresh. The widespread phenomenon of longevity, which is after all a completely new occurrence in our part of Europe, confronts us with hidden and surprising challenges. And we in turn always respond according to our – no doubt basically somewhat inflexible – psychic make-up. Realising this or not.

In modern societies the number of divorces has been rising at an alarming rate for a long time. A new model of the family has been established where the children from the first marriage of the father grow up with those from the second. Some are surprised, others simply wring their hands or attempt to forbid this. And in the case of Mr P., after a brief meeting with these ghosts, it would appear to him that such divorces are simply a natural answer to longevity – that in fact, not that much has changed. For after all, not so long ago the average marriage lasted 10, perhaps 15 years. Then it collapsed. Not as a result of divorce. As a result of death – also a form of leaving.

Perhaps the simple fact of living with one person longer than ten years is terribly difficult? And therefore, when *kicking the bucket* was not an option, people cast themselves away? For in fact there is no longer a reason to live together any longer. The reasons that joined people in the first place when they were twenty-something, usually are not particularly important for those about to turn forty. These are in fact totally different people, who have other needs, other social roles and other interests. And if they hadn't been able to follow a similar road together (which is rare), then one day they wake up next to someone who had departed already a long time ago. Divorce then becomes only a formality.

And after all there is the added matter of children. Those unfortunate children from 'divorced' homes! Is this not a new, dramatic phenomenon? Well, certainly not new. Already a hundred years ago the majority of fifteen-year-olds had only one parent, if not in some cases, no parents. Their mothers had died, fathers had taken another wife known as a step-mother and all somehow continued to manage. So in this regard little has changed – but at the same time a lot as well. Mr. P. doesn't think that it is good to be a child from a divorce but at the same time that there is too much drama today put into this situation.

Living through separation with those who are most important, the closest, is probably part of fate's script and whether the cause is death or a court verdict, does not change very much. As for the child's emotional life this always equates to being abandoned, which somehow has to be accepted.

Perhaps the greatest and most dramatic, however, change that longevity has brought is those blessed with longevity. In the previous centuries the departure enforced by death left at best one person who had to manage with life in the future. In addition, the real burdens of that life as a matter of practicality imposed a repeated act of union. A totally different story these days. Two lonely people appear who often are not able to accept that they have lost something – so they too are not prepared to risk again.

They fill their life with work, nervous activity and often, sacrifice themselves for their child. Work and child, child and work – filling every moment, every day of life. A lack of close relationship with someone who would be at a similar stage of life, who would also, say, have left five years to retirement. This lack is important. For afterwards the child departs for their own life, the final day of work nears and suddenly, a void. Not a thing. In fact no one. Nothing is important now and time passing slowly is filled by the talking heads of TV. And life shall continue still for a long, long time.

Perhaps it was worth – at the end of the day – dying in battle, or at childbirth?

Will men survive?

In reality the anxiety over masculinity is not fully justified. It is still the case that male supremacy remains a fact. Even in the context of Western culture it is women who fight for equal rights and not vice versa. And it is a culture that is perhaps the most gyno-centric out of all known to Mr. P., not counting of course those legendary matriarchal cultures.

There are, however, a certain number of facts that cast doubt as to the future fate of men. In themselves they are perhaps not of great consequence – but when put together....

Fact one – biological. For some time doctors and biologists have observed a fall in fertility and capacity of male sperm cells in various species. This affects man, alligators, birds and many others. No one knows for sure why this is so but the fact remains that more and more often men have less sperm cells so as to fertilise women – and when they do, these cells under a microscope are somewhat deformed and that in the case of alligators and fish the reproductive organs do not develop, as is the case with birds.

Ecologists maintain that this is the effect of an excessive, unnatural dissemination of female hormones in nature known as estrogens, as well associate substances. And where do these estrogens come from? Well, from two main sources. Foremost in regions with a high civilisation level where there are increasing numbers of women at an advanced age.

For women live longer. And if it were not enough that they wish to live longer, they wish to be women longer. At a certain stage they begin – for this purpose – to add artificial hormones to their organism. Female of course. In the form of injections, pills, creams. And these hormones, those that come to leave their bodies, add to the sum of sewage, then rivers, seas, clouds, rain and all of nature itself.

That there is some truth to this is the fact that alligators in particular have suffered. Thus alligators, particularly those subject to intensive research, live in Florida. And who lives in Florida apart from alligators? Almost all the pensioners – and of course females ones – from the East Coast of the USA. Thus if the theory presented above is well founded, then the swamps of Florida have to be swimming with female hormones. And so it all stacks up. In fact these alligators have been found to have unusually frequent incidents of receded (apologies for the word) testicles and in general, if they manage to reproduce, it is only by some miracle.

This is the first fact. Now the second – also biological. Some time ago scientists learnt to clone – that is to multiply a fertilised egg cell. From this one cell it is possible to produce a million fertilised cells. For the purpose of these cells changing into human beings, now only women are required, who accept these cells into their wombs (apologies for the word) and then give birth to children. Men are no longer particularly required. When, however, scientists learn to clone unfertilised egg cells – this is possible and is known as (apologies again) as virgin birth – men will be absolutely dispensable. The human species will be able to continue in its feminine form

And finally fact three, socio-biological. Thus in the kingdom of mammals, to which we belong, the male usually not only has a defined role in the reproductive process, but also a very specific social one. This role more or less depends on ensuring – thanks to the advantage of physical strength – the safety of female individuals and his young progeny. And so it was ever thus among humans up to the 19th century. Men were indispensable in social terms.

And now no longer are. Women manage splendidly with all that comes their way – management, construction, production, gastronomy and flying. If in some fields their role is small, as for example in waging wars, this is an insignificant, incomprehensible atavism. The remainder of humanity is concerned with eliminating war as a form of rivalry between people.

A so we have the full picture. First men are not required to ensure their species endures biologically. Second, they are dispensable in social terms. Third, there arises the biological process that eliminates them (apologies – us, thinks Mr. P.). In the natural world it is usually the case that if a particular species becomes redundant, it disappears. In principle, nature cannot afford anything that is redundant. Therefore, whether we like it or not, at some point in the future men shall become increasingly rare – it shall be increasingly more difficult to meet a full-blooded specimen and subsequently, men will only be found in textbooks and museums. Unless of course women establish reservations for men.

Behind this joke, however, there is an entirely serious question lurking. To what extent does our species still abide by the general laws of nature, especially evolution ? For if so, then men are in reality under threat. Or perhaps not. Perhaps it is the case, as in many other matters, we as a species create our own human reality. And in this reality, gender is not important – a purely biological condition – but various, completely other forms of condition. Human, specifically human. If so then we stand a chance. And do not have to be concerned so much, with the benders of gender.

Curriculum vitae

Curriculum vitae. The course of life. Resonates profoundly. All the more that the CV is the history of life narrated as an account of battles for survival. A history narrated with a purpose.

In telling a tale, the narrator always sets themselves an aim of some sort. Stories though are best told at a time when the aim is the tale itself. The aim of the CV is only to gain the opportunity for a job interview. In principle the CV is the first part of the statement in such a dialogue. Our tale will determine whether the reader and potential interlocutor will turn his gaze away from us and examine another's progress in life, or the opposite – to become more familiar with the narration of our life. We are therefore in the situation of someone, who on finding themselves in a large group, attempts to stand out.

Therefore the importance of not so much the content but how it's conveyed. Before even the addressee of our CV can get to know us better and assess our undoubted talents and attributes, they have to notice us in the first place. In addition, noticing us, we cannot afford to deter them. The first impression is vital. Hair freshly groomed. The skirt to the knee but not too short, without ostentation. Just as the course of life. It should be reasonably compact, though not too laconic. Life ought to be bright, clear and coherent. In visual terms, one's record should be presented as meritorious and important facts should be made bold or underlined such that when read, they can be found easily.

If these rules are followed then the most vital information can be given to the reader. This says that the candidate belongs to the same world. That they know the rules that govern them and won't pull a rabbit out of the hat. That they are a person the reader might consider as: 'Someone we can trust, someone that speaks the same language we do'.

The order in which the course of life should be told, is the reverse of chronological order. We begin from *now*, then, moving away in time, facts and events are outlined, which are responsible for this *now*. For in essence the most important is this *now* and the future. The only justification of the past existing is that it gives birth to the future.

The coherence of life should express itself in the fact that its episodes come to form a unified, linear organised whole. This proves that we know how to plan our life. That it does not dictate to us like a helpless child. A child that cannot organise its hierarchy of aims, is continually taken by surprise by various events and can be distracted by a passing starling, a cat licking its kittens in the sun or the tribulations of a fly faced with a windowpane. While the little bucket and plastic cast – thanks to which a three-year-old child's work of posterity shall arise – will be forgotten in the sandpit.

Thus the world in which the tracks of life fall into place in a CV is the world organised according to a hierarchy of aims. Only the aims attain the status of important elements. The *curriculum vitae* narration shows what aims a person – an absolute subject – sets, what they do to accomplish them, where they are headed. In general it reveals that they control their life. If a person has not managed to control their life, if they would not be an absolute subject – how would they otherwise find it possible to control anything at all, to influence the world out there?

The author and at the same time main protagonist of the CV has to self-ordain the status of a deity, one that can influence their fate. An amazing valour. For not even the Greek gods had power over the Moirai, had to reconcile themselves with their verdict. Only Zeus at times could change the nature of things. And here such courage and in addition, viewed as if a totally natural course of events. As if the author of the CV pronounced: 'It's obvious that my life does what it's told'. Naturally for the potential interlocutor this is an attractive attribute. When it's all said and done, it is a pleasure to make contact with a deity.

Problem being only that this trait has ceased to draw attention – in fact because it has become banal. Rather its lack stands out. If someone would write of their life: 'I tasted failure which forces me to reconsider what I have been doing up to now', or: 'For many months I have eaten, slept, observed the world, evenings drank beer without much desire for anything until one Friday my brother-in-law proposed a lift to work'. This no doubt would cause a discouraging impression – someone who lacks godly traits, who is simply an object, a small boat on the stormy waves of fate. Someone of this calibre will not establish a factory or a chain of shops – out of nothing.

The author's sense of almighty power is one where they must tempered by their awareness that they are a part of a greater whole, where their agency, actions – link and merge with that of others. It is only these streams and rivers of activity that come to unite, which constitute an aim that we strive for. Those who forget this will not be seen as a good employee. And it should not be forgotten that all the time this is a matter of searching for employment.

A good deal many of us have to labour with the narrative form of a *curriculum vitae*, particularly those who are the fundament of society – the middle class. For the *curriculum vitae* the narrative and natural context is the labour market – that is why, it is the way it is. The problem being that in the experience of most, no other situation forces us to organise the most important facts of life in a rational, thought-out whole, organised according to a paradigm other than one growing from the stand at a bazaar like Thackeray's *Vanity Fair*.

For the seriously faithful such an occasion might be confession – but how many are there out there? And does the Church in fact encourage this? To what extent does the philosophy imposed by the labour market remain the only chance to narrate our life? And how does it influence the self-awareness many of us have?

Marek Hłasko, an East-European writer living in the middle of the 20th century, argued that he perfected his style and self-consciousness on the literary form of denunciation. Denunciation is also a form of dialogue, one addressed to a specific 'receiver' – only in a different social reality, one of dictatorship. Of some comfort is that regardless of the limitations of its context and function, the *curriculum vitae* will perhaps also become a work-in-progress making possible a process of self-knowing. In addition, their view of the world will – despite all – be somewhat more optimistic than the one shaped in the school of 'dobbers'.

Cows

Do you remember the mad cow disease epidemic? At the time Mr. P. wondered why in fact cows? Donors of *filet mignon* – that poetry of taste à *la* meat, fried in thick two or even three centimetre slices on a pan wrought red hot – with a flake of butter placed on top, so the meat would stay moist. The only donors of a side of roast beef, a massive, juicy hunk of red meat – the essence of life-giving strength along which pink blood streams down the blade of a long knife. A special instrument for cutting roast, a distant cousin of the sacrificial knife that once evoked the same sleeping power in haunches yet to be quartered. Hiding, like a secret, graceful small leaves of *carpaccio,* jokingly known as small tongues of taste whose encounter with green olive oil and several small capers will always come as a surprise to those for whom slaughtered cattle are a sign of brute strength rather than subtlety.

Why then did it in fact affect those creatures who were granted to us so that we feast our weakness on their strength – so that we, using their patient mild-manneredness, could ingest their body and with this something else, something permanently tied to our culture of Theseus killing the Minotaur.

Maybe this affects us less, thinks Mr. P., Slavs enamoured of that pink soft body of swine – not as blooded and massive but rather provincial, delicate after roasting with that unrepeatable lardiness glistening on its surface. The western world, however, proud of its herds, farms and abattoirs – the West was hit by a thunderbolt. Florence cutlets on the bone – in Italy the consumption of beef fell in some regions as much as 90 per cent! *Fondue Bourguignonne* – French veterinary authorities are forcing farmers to kill the great, white, gentle calves and their bodies are burnt in industrial stoves. German sausages – cast with suspicious looks by yesterday's fans, those who start to think what has been minced, added to *Leberwurst.*

Unsuccessfully do we try to replace beef with a substitute. The incredible demand for poultry, millions of chickens stilettoed with a long thin blade – does not appear, however, capable of filling the hiatus in the menu. How many chickens are required to balance the lack of a young bull of the *Charentaise* breed? And this is not only a matter of kilograms. Does the sum of their suffering not exceed that of cattle – so as to meet our hunger, a single suffering has to be multiplied several hundred times. On the other hand, chicken soup and roast chicken legs – how much longer can this go on? What then is the white meat of the chicken that disintegrates so against the grey fibres of a bull's muscles. It has no substance.

The large birds are making a career: turkeys, peacocks. Their legs and breasts to some degree can substitute the massive roast. The start of the third millennium, an epoch in which peacocks settled Europe. How will the hills of Burgundy look without peacefully grazing cattle, white pools against a background of green, a sea of black eyes of never-ending goodnaturedness. Instead, groups of grey two-legged non-fliers with long necks. Yuk!! After all, a bull kidnapped Europa from Crete, not a peacock!

We have destroyed it with too much love – for their meat. Too much desire, faith, greed. It appeared to us that cows could do us no harm. Swine, bearers of cholesterol, yes. Sheep, always a little suspect and in addition too skinny. Cows, however, motherly, peaceful with no hint of rebellion, laying their heads down for the chopping block. We thought that there will always continue a great milling mill – bull, cow, cow-shed, calves, grain, axe-head, T-bone and again cow-shed, and again grain. But we wished too soon, too much, we trusted too much that this production line can be developed ad infinitum. As ecologists say, we have taught it cannibalism. We have infected it with madness, a specifically human ailment.

At present we are experiencing disillusionment and anger. We shower it with invectives – angry, mad ones; after all though, they suffer incomparably more than we do. For they have let us down. For we thought that they will always look at us with buttery eyes under long eyelashes and agree to an eternal order of the world. That they will be an inexhaustible and goodnatured source of beef and rum steaks – with their compliance shall reinforce our false sense that everything is in order. And they suddenly start swaying or jump wildly sideways, streaming foam from their snout and meet death. We can no longer trust them. Degenerates. In every piece of their body they may hide a curse.

And it is only eaters of hamburgers who do not take this overly to heart. McDonalds full as usual. But do eaters of hamburgers take anything to heart at all?

Chopsticks and fork

Roland Barthes in reflecting on the essence of Japanese civilisation has devoted
a great deal of attention to the matter of chopsticks – examining the structural
opposition between the fork and chopstick – thus noting and recording the
specificity of a culture that invented such different instruments for appeasing
hunger. There is, however, something Barthes did not see. Thus, regardless of
how many cultures we examine, we shall find a surprisingly poor range of
utensils that serve to transfer food to one's mouth.

There exist hundreds of languages used, hundreds of different ways to kill
and many ways to raise buildings. The art of making love practiced in various
cultures shows such numerous techniques that no matter how long one searches,
something new can always be found. When it comes to the technique of
transferring food to the mouth, however, there is almost nothing to speak of. In
reality there are three basic methods.

One could venture the thesis that eating, part of human physiology, has its
natural laws that define the extent of a possible variety in this respect. In
addition, one could also argue there is nothing to examine here. That is not so.
Food is an act for which we devote usually a considerable amount of attention
and time. Moreover, in every culture the practice of eating is governed highly by
norms and regulations. It is therefore one of the spheres in which there is a
meeting of the biological with the cultural in man. During such an encounter
there is the threat of primal forces of nature being released, disturbing our
customs and that is why this sphere always draws so much of our attention.

In the European tradition, how we behave at the table equates with to what
degree we are able to make use of several utensils that serve in the transferral of
food from the plate to the mouth – immediately placing us in the social
hierarchy. There is nothing more embarrassing during an elegant reception as
the sense of helplessness in confrontation with knives, small forks and spatulae
placed around the plate.

Transferring food to the mouth is therefore a social activity of significance,
one circumscribed by numerous taboos. This must be important. The above
three families of utensils that serve this activity are: European (fork, knife and
spoon), The 'East' (chopsticks, knife and spoon) and other regions (hand and
usually knife).

The first matter that draws one's attention is that the difference in the above
is only in moving bite-sized objects to the mouth. The knife though is a common
element in practically all cultures. Not by accident. The flint knife, next to the
hand axe is the most ancient of tools found by archaeologists in relation to
prehistoric man. The function of breaking into smaller pieces and dividing into

bite-size pieces is absolutely a fundamental activity in eating. Here man, devoid of fangs and claws has to use a cutting utensil. A biological conditioning, one that is natural and which still dominates.

After separating a piece of food it is necessary to somehow bring it to the mouth. And here a difference arises, here culture modifies a simple, natural activity. Why at this particular moment? Perhaps the act of introducing something to the organism is much more revealing, intimate than tearing apart, cutting off – an activity in fact that belongs to hunting.

Humans, in opening their mouth, reveal themselves, show their interior. Moreover, it is a moment when it allows the world to overcome the boundary between I and non-I. A moment that is threatening, dangerous, in which every person has to for a while be weak, open to all, which in this moment can break into the interior. A literal threat, associated with this break-in – the possibility of eating poison or something that contains bacteria – should not blind us to the symbolic threat that stimulates in every living being the blurring of the boundary separating it from the outside world.

The routine of leading the piece of food to the mouth therefore reflects to some degree the relationship to the non-I – how the opening to the world is experienced in a given culture. The simplest is to bring the food by hand. That is how the majority of primal peoples do it. Maybe this is tied to a still strong bond experienced in the surrounding reality or rather, the lack of a clear barrier between reality and the I, a barrier that arises in so called cultures of extended duration.

Though among historical cultures that have endured over millennia, there are those in which this style of eating has been preserved. One possible example is the civilisation of south India, where rice is eaten with the hand. The problem here is the preservation of cleanliness – real and symbolic – tools that allow to cross the boundary between I and non-I. It is possible to maintain a true cleanliness by carefully washing hands, though the matter of symbol is not that straightforward. Islam resolves this problem by transferring the washing of hands into the sphere of *sacrum*. Hinduism otherwise. It establishes that there is a hand marked for 'clean' activities, the right and one for unclean, the left. Food can be brought only by the right hand. The left serves everything that is related to 'taking out'.

Perhaps in fact the resolution of the problem of the purity of a utensil serving to overcome the above mentioned boundary resulted in the appearance of chopsticks and forks. If so, then it certainly shows that this problem appeared in the cultures of Europe and Asia at various periods. In Asia chopsticks have been in use since prehistoric times, while the fork became widespread in Europe at the threshold of modern civilisation. Why is it, however, that all the south of our globe eats with their hands and that utensils serving for food appeared in cultural centres situated relatively to the north? One possible explanation is the need to consume hot meals in a cold climate that did not lend themselves to eating with hands.

Barthes in deliberating on the opposition between a fork and chopsticks, notes that there is a totally different relation between the utensil and the piece of food that is taken by it. In fact, only a small bite is taken by chopsticks – using them to eat is something rather prepossessing. In addition, it is relatively difficult. Eating Asian dishes with the aid of chopsticks is an art form whereby the artist-eater subtly and with care moves into the dimension of taste elements of the canvas that is a table full of many varied dishes. Chopsticks force one to concentrate, do not allow meals to be taken lightly. That is why the consumption of works of Chinese cuisine or *sushi* with the help of a fork always result in the loss of a certain charm, which is integral to this type of meal.

The fork therefore is a tool of violence. Its initial function best represents the means of using forks: stabbing, grabbing but not taking. A European that eats roast still conquers the world: makes an appearance, strips away, immobilises. After all, the initial shape of a fork fully matched its function: two long prongs stemming from the hilt. It was only with the passing of the centuries that the fork took over one more function from the spoon – that of scooping.

Why didn't something else appear and why did humankind limit itself to inventing only a few simple utensils? Is it the case that the entire spectrum of approaches to eating was limited to these? Why, there is the oyster knife and pliers for crabs that do not change the basic choice that we are faced with: chopsticks, fork or hand – and the maternal spoon. And is that all? Those who have learnt to effectively use chopsticks know how much this changes the experience itself of food. Thus, maybe there is some mysterious irreparable loss in the fact that we are condemned to only these few utensils.

The odds of risk

Coloured multi-lotto balls, marked with numbers, circle in a transparent drum, hypnotising millions of viewers with their rattle. Those glued to television screens are already counting their winnings in their head, settling in villas on the Caribbean, sailing yachts or simply contemplate legs of ham, huge gateaux, luxury boots and jackets – and all of this awaits them somewhere in the fall of numbers that a honey-voiced presenter shall call out.

The lottery monopoly, right to earn by exploiting the hunger for winnings, is a fantastic source of income for the state. This has the capacity to top-up the budget thanks to selling hope of a sudden change of fortune, a great *sting*, into something that has no right to occur. The demand for hope is immense and the cost of a single lottery ticket, rather insignificant.

Though it remains a mystery for Mr. P., this deep attachment by a huge group of people to a voluntary tax. A permanent, additional tax! Naturally, out of these monies the monopoly builds stadiums and other facilities but in fact the vast majority of those taking part, if asked whether they wish to be taxed for example for the development of a skating ring, would protest in outrage. At the same time these same people stand in queues to buy a lottery ticket.

Human consciousness most eagerly oscillates between certainty and contradiction, avoiding everything that stands in between. This can already be seen at school when learning to calculate the sum of probability comes with great difficulty to children, even though in a formal sense it is not at all the most complicated section of mathematics. It can also be seen in the two-thousand-year tradition of logic that bases on truth and falsehood, not taking into account that which in fact exists only to a certain degree.

Awareness, remarks Husserl, likes and wishes to present what is given, with a puffed up sense of certainty. It is so and so and if not, then not at all. The table I see before me is simply there. It cannot 'be' with an equal probability for instance to 75%. This form of logic, incontestable in relation to a table and every other material object present in the here and now is not reliable in the face of everything that is not an object. For that matter, physicists dealing with statistics maintain that tables also exist only with a defined probability.

In addition, the attractiveness of number games is based on a subtle permeation in human consciousness of certainty and risk. Everyone knows that practically always someone takes the winnings. Almost every week it can be seen that someone has those lucky six numbers – the lottery is therefore a near certainty. Nobody thinks about the millions of losers. The incapacity to possibly imagine these great numbers is here the basis of illusion, pleasure personified – after all if they can win, so can I!

We live in a world of the village – 'large' signifies for us 100, 200 people, so if 50 have already won, then this subjective feeling of my own chances grow to completely sensible fractions and percentages. In total opposition to a rational account that shows the disproportions between these 50 and let's say 8 million that in reality *throw the dice*. For '8 million' does not exist in our grasp of the arithmetic, cannot be represented.

It can therefore be suspected that the popularity of number games is tied to this fallibility of the human mind, its inability to differentiate the things that exist more than others. That is, explain everything in terms of a peculiar nonsense. Will this, however, suffice? It shall not. There also remain desires.

In the modern world the estimation of real probabilities of repetitive events has become the profession and science of the economy. As in the lottery monopoly, it's a milking cow for insurance companies that change the uncertainty of events into the certainty of payouts. Insurance ingratiates itself to the above mentioned traits of the human mind that wish to function in the sphere of certainty. Broadening the field in which every unfortunate event can be neutralised, insurance creates a false sense of protection over fate gone wrong.

Illusory? Yes, indeed illusory. Not taking lightly the values of a sense of safety arising from the fact that for instance, for a stolen car there is compensation, it should be noted that misfortune always finds a means to slip into peoples' lives. It has a million faces and an infinity of ways. Thousands of European Jews, insuring their life in Swiss associations, experienced this tragic irony first hand.

The ability to foresee extraordinary events, in reality unrepeatable, is an altogether different matter. It is laden with particular difficulty and does not allow to be placed in the confines of routine models. And at the same time, the majority of truly important events that change the course of life and fate, slip out of the daily, routine machinery of daily existence. Therefore the gift of assessing with what probability events will occur that normally do not, is the source of prestige, money and foremost, power. This is a talent that makes great statesmen and financial sharks. They have to in fact foresee what events among many possible will turn out as the one and only. Those whose existence *ex post* will appear simply obvious but which earlier was only a shadow among hundreds of other shadows.

Those who are not able, have to remain in the circle of continually repeated activity, checked, giving certain results that are not threatened by mistakes. Though they dream of exceptions to the rule. They too would like to control the unforeseen. So like the protagonist of a funny commercial addressed to inhabitants burdened by life in a middle-sized East European country, dream of donning Napoleon's uniform. And plan strategies of casting numbers so they can finally get a grip on fate, one that continues to be so elusive.

Workaholic

The workaholic, as we know, is always on the run. Even when asleep. Their mind then does not rest but is preparing strategies – maybe tactics – future challenges. The dreams of Workaholics usually are of some tiring vision of offices where they cannot find the right room, right place, right person and so in the face of this all embracing numbness, nothing is as it should be. Fortunately, for their own sake, workaholics do not usually remember their dreams. When they have time to do so they are busy elsewhere.

A workaholic's breath is fast and rather shallow. Dog specialists call this type of breath panting or hyper-panting. The workaholic continually pants (dog-like). Though as far as dogs are concerned, this type of breathing is tied to the need to cool the organism, which is aided by intensive streaming of saliva in the open snout. In the case of a human being, which no doubt the workaholic is, they have another cause – the breath is quick for everything is done quickly. Workaholics believe that by maintaining the organism in a state of readiness, allowing any work to be undertaken at any moment, demands a continual dose of large amounts of energy, which as we know is related to a generous inhalation of air.

As far as the real need for the moment, this breath is though a little fast. So as not to faint under the influence of being overwhelmed by oxygen, the workaholic makes their breath shallow. This has an additional, huge advantage. Shallow breath allows for a firming up of all of the trunk muscles. Thanks to this, the workaholic's torso becomes a powerful impervious armour that protects from a breakdown. And a workaholic could very well break down. There is after all so much work...

Panting though, leads to a desiccation of the mucous membrane. The workaholic therefore is endlessly thirsty. And drinks without end. Mineral water, juices, coffee, mixed drinks. More on mixed drinks later – here we shall stop at coffee. Coffee is irreplaceable to the workaholic. Usually this is justified by continual tiredness caused by a heavy, to say the least, work routine. Thanks to this, workaholics can drink litres of coffee daily without any pangs of conscience. Coffee though, has other functions. It wakes the organism, causing artificial stimulation, allows without continually lapsing to run fast forward in thought beyond the present moment to plan, to design, to be elsewhere. The mind of a workaholic, as in the engine of a F1 racing motorcar already first before the start, is on the highest revolutions. It's already on the race track, flies, any moment will enter the curve, though it would seem to be still here.

For a workaholic is never in their thoughts there where they presently are. They are not present directly in the available reality. This defines what is perhaps its most important characteristic. They see the world through the lens of their daydreams which they call aims. And as a consequence what is directly under their nose they do not see. They vault over them so that their mind can devote itself to a new scheme of things that are set. Its own new order.

Therefore in fact it is difficult to make human contact with a workaholic. When they speak to you at the same time they think three steps ahead. Look into your eyes but do not see you, do not hear your answer – the only important thing is their plans for tonight. When you go for a walk – he, listening to your words on the colours of autumn, turns his thoughts forward to the fact that it will be necessary to fill the car up with petrol. And when both of you are eating supper, his thoughts – let us continue to speak about a male workaholic – are already with his hand, which allows him to undo the zipper of your dress.

Though in the matter of sex, a workaholic has substantial problems. This is the case, for sexual responses cannot be planned or controlled – they demand in contrast, an empathy of real experience. When his body touches the body of another person, when their skins twin-like meet, the workaholic's thoughts are already with the fireplace that he planned for their mutual nest. The thought of the fireplace is though too weak an aphrodisiac and thus the workaholic suffers a defeat. And later often, during subsequent tactile encounters, the workaholic is already thinking only of his potential defeat. And that is why sex is not at all a favourite pastime of workaholics.

They prefer monitors – television or computer. Especially TV. Therefore, from their point of view, just like they – and a 'twin' spirit can be trusted fully. Television has everything planned, leads you by the hand from one image to the next and wishes for nothing in return. Thanks to it, there is no need to make contact with the unexpected. Before turning the TV on, a workaholic's thoughts have wiped all and sundry, and in this way only they and their daydreams remain. Now there is 'another' construction of daydreams, construction of images presenting themselves on the screen, which wipe out the workaholic's grasp of the present, allowing for a moment to suspend 'being'. It is then the workaholic can relax. Only then.

Workaholism, as every 'ism', is considered in our times as something to be avoided. An addiction to work, thanks to which – for what it's worth – 100 floor skyscrapers arise, as do new fashion collections and new generations of anti-biotics, that allow finally for financiers in New York to immediately react to the jitters of the Hong Kong stock market – even though all this demands they do not get any sleep – and thus this form of addiction known in the past as conscientiousness, is seen today as an illness that needs to be treated.

No doubt because the workaholic flees directly from the reality around them. And in today's world it has become accepted to think that without a direct contact with the world, with others as well as a panting, faithful dog, you cannot be happy. That it's necessary for a moment to stop and look – at others, at human faces, at a landscape.

What races the workaholic forward is the continual feeling that 'there's something amiss'. Contemporary psychology suggests that this 'amiss' resides in their own spirit from which flow suppressed expressions of regret, frustration or anger. If the workaholic therefore only for a moment were to stop, cease to escape from the present, from reality, these expressions would wash them away – and that would be unbearable. And therefore when they wish to rest, it is simple to let the 'drama' of TV take them elsewhere or they pour themselves another cocktail, which makes their own company bearable. It is then that the workaholic forgets that they are not happy.

But does everyone have to be happy?

Here a question mark is born. For one would have to invent a world in which the condition of happiness and self satisfaction is considered as not only a fundamental human right but also responsibility. A world that demands to treat those that are otherwise unusually productive, who do not experience this condition to the full.

The workaholic belongs to another world. To the world of a related protestant asceticism as described by Max Weber. In our world where happiness is an obligation, the workaholic turns into a patient – whereas in *Weberland*, they express fully man's calling. From that point of view, it is not a problem for man – marked by original sin – to be happy. Self-satisfaction is suspect but work on the other hand, mountains of work, is a shield from all impure temptation flowing from idleness. In particular, faced with the temptation of stopping, sloth, needless contact with landscapes, art and others. From the very depths of their own reality the workaholic could reply in the words of preachers: "Not leisure and enjoyment but only activity serves to increase the glory of God, according to the definite manifestations of His will [...] Thus inactive contemplation is also valueless, or even directly reprehensible if it is at the expense of one's daily work. For it is less pleasing to God than the active performance of His will in a calling"[2]

So perhaps we should let workaholics be, let them live their life of productivity – at least to the moment when they come to us to lament on the productive life they have led.

---

2   Max Weber, *The Protestant Ethic and the Spirit of Capitalism*, New York:Scribner, 1930, p. 157, 158.

The remote control: an odyssey

A familiar motif, for example from the drawings of Roland Topor. High-rise flats like cells in a beehive. One next to the other, dozens – in great slabs of housing estates. Everywhere. In these flats, cheek by jowl, families reside. If one could, like angels from Berlin, pass from one to another, look and see, observe. When evening falls they sit in front of the TV and the above odyssey begins.

Mr W. A couch upholstered in popular postmodern, a rug on the parquet floor and in the corner opposite, a Sony Bravia television. The entire room is engulfed in semi-darkness, lit up by the coloured splashes beaming out of the screen. The windows have long assumed the blue of television and the TV pumps out colour.

Mr W. rests his hand on a coffee table in front of the couch. The hand, relaxed, holds the remote control. The fingers, witness to manicure, move freely along the number-board. The most important finger, the index, stays on the most important button – choice of channel. Mr W. does not have to look, search for the right button. Has trained for where the numbers go. The remote is placed where the beam reaches the TV receptor in a flash, and reacts accordingly.

Mr W. squeezes the remote, the beam reaches the receptor and the image on the screen changes completely. Accompanied by a sudden lapse of sound – as if a greater capacity for loss than the picture – and after a moment, words start flowing, matching the changing scenes. Mr W. with his other hand reaches for a small crystal bowl with salted peanuts. Scoops two or more, brings them to his mouth, bites, swallows and with his index finger placed on the remote, again squeezes a change of channel. The character on the screen vanishes, something completely different appears, again the sound lapses behind then quickly catches step with the image – machine gunfire fills Mr W.'s room.

Mr W. squeezes the remote for a change of channel, the image vanishes then a talking head appears, clearly excited, in a green jacket then Mr W. squeezes the remote and on the screen sun-bronzed blonds in bikinis run along the beach and the index finger momentarily wavers in its routine of up and down – Mr W. again swallows several peanuts then after a moment the squeeze of the index finger and the blonds are wiped from the screen, falling into nothingness. In their place out floats a dappled cow in delayed accompaniment that speaks of how The Cow is the symbol of bad investment in the agricultural sector, then the index finger squeezes...

Let us go then you and I to the wall's other, to Mr and Mrs Y. Sitting in front of the box in their armchairs. Mr Y. holds the remote with both hands, thumb squeezing channel after channel according to their number. With every change his wife can be heard in the dark: 'Jurek, stop it, let's watch something –

you've gone bananas!' Mr Y. though only stops for a brief moment, allowing his wife to bear witness to an opinion voiced and hidden behind a dappled cow on the futility of investment. Another squeeze of the thumb, then bikini blonds, machinegun fire, a man in a green jacket and finally, the hysterical scream of Mrs Y:

'For God's sake give me that bloody **REMO-O-O-O-T!**'

Then through the floor and through the ceiling of the flat below. No sound. Darkness. TV off. They are out.

The remote, allowing to skip from channel to channel – in particular if the cable network or satellite antenna offers several hundred programmes – has a surprisingly hypnotic power. It can in effect, turn an ordinarily rational, intelligent person into one glued to the flashing screen and with the slightest of moves index finger changing the world out there – flowing out of the box into nothingness, giving birth to a totally different reality. Though not because it is to remain there – for after all, after a moment, even before this reality will become a part of his mindset for good, he rejects it and searches for another. Searches? Is that searching? Why do we resort to such absurdity and *to boot*, find an unrepeatable pleasure in so doing? A pleasure destroying, according to Robert Putnam, our societies?

There is a half answer that compares the above to mechanical amusement, akin to turning the kaleidoscope. Above all, a person glued to the TV screen, remote in hand is usually able to recognise the meaning of the images that appear. And only then, when this meaning becomes understood, do they pass to the next channel. It is therefore not only a matter of flashing *to* and *fro*. In the end, every one of us looking into the kaleidoscope also processes the images that appear into something complete, finished, brimming with particularity. And only then, with such a complete picture internalised, do we pass to the next formation.

The TV picture is, however, something more than a once-off dimensional form in a kaleidoscope. It also develops in time, in dialogue with the world out there, creating it and drawing the viewer into its orbit. They who understand the meaning of the image begin to 'reside' in the reality, which that image represents. And only if they be Odysseus of the remote control, if only they reside in it, cast it off at once, searching for another. Why?

When the image is established, when we already know the point, who shoots at whom, or what he sings, when the unknown becomes the known, impatience suddenly appears. This is not it. This is not what I'm looking for. Maybe something more interesting can be found elsewhere. An impatience and irritation which everydayness arouses, impatience which is the source of a rather commonly experienced feeling that 'everywhere is fine where I'm not', can find expression where one small movement of the finger is sufficient, so as to change reality. The remote endows the feeling of great power.

Or maybe the simple fact is that the hidden need for nomadism practically extinguished in us, ascribed to some small domicile, propels us to embark on this odyssey: the TV remote control.

Weather forecast

The first, fundamental experience of *sacrum*, Mirce Eliade discovers in experiencing the open heavens. Man, who is confronted in the abyss filled with stars, in the hugeness and void, experiences something of a mystery, one difficult to define. Something that brings to mind thoughts of the deities. Later that dimension begins to be filled with storms, thunderbolts, rain, fog, a crowd of clouds and a malicious drizzle, gales of wind and light zephyrs.

Each of these phenomena defines the world in which man lives, changes him, imbues with an unrepeatable character. Each assumes a name. Sacrum appears in the thunderbolts of Zeus, in Odin's anger, in the puffed up cheeks of Boreas and Zephyr. Man, from day to day meets with the power of one of these gods. Once when leaving home in the cold and unfriendly world of winter, another time taking shelter against the fury of the Tempest, or attempting to wait out the damp and greyness of time when it seems as if all the gods had forgotten mere mortals.

Later still man forgets the names of deities. Only the weather forecast remains. Mr P.'s lady friend, Jagoda, who begins each day of work with a cup of coffee, complains about something 'hanging' in the air. She detests the weather. No matter what mood she's in, the weather is always hostile and unwilling. This time Jagoda has her fair share of argument – a hanging, decomposing greyness enveloping the city has practically turned everyone's mood dark.

The weather forecast is one of the most popular programmes on television, the most viewed site on the Web. It attracts young and old before the monitor, the educated and those not, *city-zens* and those from the village and even the oldest of highlanders – for whom it is absolutely a waste – they already know what the weather will be like. Mothers watch the weather so they know how to dress their child for school tomorrow and the intrepid in the Tatra Mountains, so as to decide whether to climb the notorious Mnich peak or not.

Thanks the weather forecast we all know there exist highs and lows. Rarely does anyone understand what this in truth means but every evening it is possible to learn that the low over the Azores is pressing the weakened highs over the Ukraine and the fronts that accompany them result in many of us worsening in mood and irritability in general. When behind the wheel you need to be careful. The gods are not by our side, they demand sacrifice.

The relation between states of spirit and those of the skies, between our moods and the sun and rain is obvious. Despite all this that we have shuttered ourselves in, houses and air-conditioned cars, the mysterious deities – Highs, Lows and of course Fronts – reach for us with their hands and do as they wish. They bring us energy and take it away, cheer us up and sadden, then irritate. We can blame them for having a bad day, distaste for the eight hours in the office. They are of course also responsible for arguments with the wife but, at times, we thank them for an unearned dollop of joy.

This relationship between the changeability of the world of feelings and moods, and the changes in the environment that surrounds us is encapsulated by Georges Simenon – a favourite of Mr P. – in the tales of Inspector Maigret. Finely detailed information on the subject of weather – the April sun casting a golden shimmer over the streets of Paris, the August sun of pest-like heat waves or the winter freezing mist which gobbles up shadows – all create an atmosphere of tales that are about to be. Further, this certain something that arises in the atmosphere has an effect on what people do, delineates the nature of events. It is their canvas and gives them meaning.

Just maybe it is difficult for us to come to terms with the unjustified changeness of our inside world, just maybe we do not wish to learn the true causes of this. That is why it is with such care that we follow the skirmishes of the elements around us, look for words that shall relate to our trepidations out there.

The words recording our immediate environment, the atmosphere filled with the amicable and the hostile, the cold and the hot, the ubiquitous and the almighty that come to be the canvas, context, the final hiding place for mysterious forces that at any moment have an influence over our life. The phenomena of climate remind us of the limitations of our strength. From time to time a river that has broken its banks, a great freeze or epidemic – all show us how little it takes to be helpless, again.

Plague

First come the news one after the other – so and so is ill, another is bed-ridden – the whole family is affected. Then people one by one in our closest circle begin to suffer. The secretary at work. Mother-in-law. Friend. The kids. One begins to realize that one is carefully monitoring the organism, searching for symptoms – slight headache, backache, which only yesterday seemed to be in fact a harmless burden of one's age. All now are clear reminders, pulsating, forcing to ask the question: 'Is it now me? My turn?'

Finally, the first jump of temperature and humble resignation, even relief – it has begun, now just to keep one's head above water...

The flu that of late ran through the town several times was particularly troublesome. It began with a general severance of normal functions and a high temperature, then often a cough followed, sore throat and then the infection travelled upwards, attacking the sinuses and turning into a runny catarrh accompanied by a headache or travelling down, into pneumonia.

It would be easiest to become infected in the first phase of the disease – often when the symptoms were still not clear. After all this is the universal course of all epidemics. In truth, the one that presents danger is the one who appears as the healthy – then transmitting the breath of the disease. When, however, it's mark becomes completely clear and thus others begin to flee, then in fact contact is a great deal less unsafe.

In writing *A Journal of the Plague Year* about the Great Plague In London, Daniel Defoe also points out this detail and demonstrates the important consequences of this fact. Foremost, a growing mutual suspicion. It is not only so that one searches oneself for the first symptoms. When coming closer to someone who is sniffling or has reddened eyes, immediately there is the thought whether by chance this is someone that shall give me the 'stigma'. 'Please just keep away from me', says the secretary. Two days later she is sniffling and has reddened eyes. And is looking, accusingly, for the guilty one.

The disease after all, spreads in fact when there are still no symptoms. When those who have it sense only a little hint of suspicion, a shiver, a sudden headache. This in fact, let us repeat, causes an increase in suspicion. For some have that 'something', others not. So it's necessary to separate the two from each other – find something that permits to meet those that are safe and avoid those that are not. There is no sign though, marking one group from the other. Man, a herd animal, at a time of contagion stands before the following dilemma: only isolation ensures complete safety, but no one can withstand complete isolation. Thus we are prone to the continual risk of meeting someone that shall pass on the 'stigma'. An epidemic bears witness to the hidden threat always embedded in the human need for Others.

Daniel Defoe spends entire days, often without purpose, restlessly in his room where he has stored reserves of food for a week. In the end he leaves, breathing in a mixture of fear and relief, consoling himself with the thought: 'If the good Lord decided that He should keep me in good health, then nothing can happen to me...' Though, as he himself asks, how are we to know what the good Lord has decided?

The choice to isolate oneself completely or to expose to potential disease takes on dramatic dimensions when the disease signifies a risk of death. In the age of the flu only the elderly in general avoid leaving their home. For them therefore the flu is a deadly disease. The remainder – we take upon ourselves the risk, keeping though a tad further, one from the other.

Dilemma: isolation or risk is really great for those whose closeness to Others is ensured through love in the bodily sense. Here the choice between extreme trust and extreme danger is again relevant. The AIDS disease lacks a certain trait though, necessary so we'd in the human dimension have experience with a real 'disease' – mass proportions and widespread experience. On the northern hemisphere those infected with the HIV virus are but a microscopic number relative to the remainder. And that is why the psychological reaction is a typical one for a threatening minority and not a reaction to something that affects all – an epidemic, death's herald.

This commonality, essential for an epidemic, as well human response to it, turns a great disease into a privileged metaphor of existence. In his notes the narrator Daniel Defoe provides weekly figures for the dead in respective London parishes. Columns of numbers. In the introduction to the Polish version of Defoe's *A Journal of the Plague*, Herling-Grudziński writes about the death of the human masses, where there is always the danger that the line will become blurred between the summing of individuals and the summing of numbers per se.

The laconic style of *The Journal* provides a counterpoint in reflection, indecision, hope and the narrator's emotions in this very column of numbers. And it is striking that the only one in truth that feels, experiences – in fact one that exists – is he who says I. Only I exists. All the others are phenomena, signs and when there are many – simply columns upon columns of numbers. Disease bears witness to a fundamental loneliness – the singleness of each of us and illusion that all the rest do exist.

At the windowpane

Falling dusk. Someone, observed by Mr P. stands at the newspaper kiosk windowpane. Grey coat, dark hair. Stares into the pane that separates from brightly lit, life out there. Their face indistinct, blurred by the layered patches of shadow, reflection of fluorescent lamps and colours echoed from magazine covers that come to fill all the space taken up by the display. There are real faces there. Each forms a rectangle it has marked out, one that is known as Claudia, or Bravo, or Elle or... All exist in their own authentic.

True faces as opposed to the one misshaped, behind a shadow, they are clearly visible, harmonious – expressing unambiguous emotions and delight us. And most of all, belong to someone. Not like the face that glances at them behind the window, an anonymous face. More – a face that could not be, for it is too weak, dependent on the street lights that at times snatch out of darkness the outline of a nose, or colour the eyes, an echo of someone's fair skin.

True faces belong to true people who are given the privilege of life. Their *esse* is *percipi*. To be is to be noticed. So they are given the privilege of life reflected and multiplied in millions of images, photographs, films, anecdotes and stories that cram our screens, sites on the web and the pages of magazines. Their names are known to everyone. Their marriages, divorces, triumphs and madcap follies allow others to strike up a dialogue with them, to share the emotions of desperation, outrage, delight or mercy. This reproduction *ad infinitum* of true life of true people allows for a moment to exist for those who cannot live their own life – for what would they fill their void with.

Thus these others come evening, mill around the television – source of true life – and watch its rise and fall, love and betrayal. It is then they can truly come alive. Engrossed in half-darkness though their faces are coloured by the TV light of another's fate. Morning though, making their way along greyed footpaths, they are not alone for the holy names of soap stars fortunately are their companions, present on magazine pages, posters on the streets, in the streaming words of radio presenters. Once more they repeat their story, examine their features, turning their attention away from nondescript houses and even more so, nondescript faces.

Perhaps for the face to be real it needs to present itself within a frame? A face without a frame does not count. As in a badly centred photograph. Kurt Vonnegut once wrote that everyone's life usually is focused on one important story. A short story. The story ends, life flows on. The remainder, the several dozen years left, is an epilogue. A period earmarked for foretelling this story to oneself. What then if no story ever took place? If one waits several dozen years for a story and it does not come? Or even if it does, it is a story – let us assume – for a 90 minute tale? Or 30 minute. Or simply for one rather unfunny joke?

The remaining time of epilogue – days, months and years – need to be devoted to foretelling oneself the lives of others.

As it is known, living the lives of others is a commonplace occurrence of our times. One needs to move ahead in the cogs of an enormous mechanism that in taking away time and will, leaves only the moment. Moments that are very brief, drained of content, crowded with a sense of almighty fatigue. Moments that must be filled with something ready-made, processed, lived through by others – those in fact created for living 'through'. It is with them that one can identify. Dance like Madonna or Lady Gaga, love like Esmeralda or Isaura and weigh justice like Forrest Gump. Who still remembers Forrest Gump?

Though do our times have a monopoly over this ailment? Or on the other hand. Is it at all possible not to live the life of others?

When Odysseus at the court of the Phaeacians' king listens to a bard recounting his own story of Odysseus, he then starts to cry. Never before had he cried. He did not cry when Cyclops gobbled up his friends, did not cry when Circes changed them into hogs. He went on. He could not afford to stop and become desperate. Could not take delight in his gamesmanship. He had to contrive. Odysseus at the Phaeacians is now a different person. He can now experience the former, one of action, a different Odysseus. As Vonnegut writes, he already lives in the epilogue. Though in the case of Odysseus, for a long time yet he was unable to reach his epilogue. For he was made for life out there. By Homer.

It is only possible to experience in full stories in which one is an observer, in truth, a listener. This is the thesis of Hannah Arendt. Only by listening to a story, even one's own but related as if it were someone else's, is it possible to gain a full awareness of its meaning. Doing, contriving, nothing is experienced. A reality is born but not its experience. In fact as far as the depth of experiencing, it is all the same whether it is one's story or not. Perhaps for the awareness of meaning, for an emotional completeness, it is better that it be a story of someone else.

Thus perhaps it's an exaggeration to be outraged at these typical families that come evening, mill around the *blinking box* so as to live through the stories told by talking heads. After all, in the past people would mill around a fire, and the elders would also speak, telling tall tales or adventures so that all listening would shake in fear, cry and empathise. With Galahad looking for the Holy Grail. With the Lady of the Lake drowning her lovers as in Esmeralda, mentioned in passing. Or with those lovers dragged into the lake. Perhaps we have to always live the life of others. Lacan would confirm and add: 'of the Other'.

There where it is said it is just like at the dawn of human history – among Australian aboriginals where no one thinks of living their own life. It would appear that the concept itself of an individual life is totally foreign to these people. It is possible to live the life of the one who creates meaning. Aborigines go walkabout, following the route of the creator of the worlds. Repeating his stories, one becomes him, at the same time confirming the world's existence. Drinking during Spring from sources, they bring water onto the earth. Departing during summer for the south, they take with them live creations so as not to be burnt by the sun. Autumn and Winter also repeat the steps of the first, for what else could have made sense?

Therefore it comes as no surprise that those who seek stories so as to live through the myths of our own times, through soaps, stories of celebrity marriages or the efforts of quiz show participants. They do not differ very much from aborigines, from the protagonists of Greek Mysteries, from the faithful passing through the way of the cross in their hearts. Human hearts were terrified when they listened to tales of the White Lady

Perhaps the only shame though is that contemporary fairy tales lack mystery. Literalness is killing them. The face from magazine covers, upright behind windowpanes, are lit by fluorescent lamps. There is no room to think. Everything is clear, defined, outlined in a bold line. Beauty, unambiguous feelings. Only someone peering at them from behind the windowpane, a face a dark splash, blurred features drowning where shadows are and the echoes of coloured lights at eye-level.

2. Melancholies and rituals

Melancholies and rituals

According to orthodox psychiatry, melancholy is the most frequent psychological indisposition. Around the globe there are around a billion depressed women and about half that number of depressed men. Thus if someone is in a state of depression they certainly have no cause to feel lonely or alienated. At hand there are melancholics aplenty. It is suffice to count to five and we can see a colleague with a fellow indisposition.

And how does one know one is in a state of depression? The question is not at all a silly one. Depression is not a toothache, nothing that can be pointed to, apart from the fact that everything is not as it should be. Depression paints the entire world in dark colours and persuades that this is in fact reality. That in reality there is no cause for laughter – and that 'others' simply are not aware of this yet.

And in the meantime it transpires that this is not at all so. Researchers have established therefore that changes to the sensitivity of post-synaptic receptors, catecholamine and 5-hydroksy-tryptophan in the brain are to blame. If a person has too little (or too much) 5-hydroksy-tryptophan, then they long for something that cannot be defined. Or they are afraid of something that cannot be defined.

The first of these conditions is known as nostalgia. A person sits, looks out into a void and pines. Only they have no idea for what. In fact they do not know that they pine. They only have nostalgia. And they sit, and they are afraid. Not knowing why. Not even knowing they are afraid. Just that it's cold somehow. The shrink knows though – they are afraid.

In melancholy it is characteristic for the person longing to refrain from doing. The more a person longs, the less they do. It is behaviour completely at odds with the course of nature. Usually every creature that longs for something, needs something, immediately reaches for it. In the case of 'simpler' creatures in general there is no place for putting aside action, which is longing. A hungry predator searches, is searching personified and when finds a victim, kills and eats it.

Maybe this 'delay', a delay into infinity, testifies to a characteristic of human aims – that at the end of the day are not possible.

Refraining from doing can be also a matter of attaining the aim, the true aim. Autonomy. Love in the end, an emotion that absolutely takes a person over, leads to losing boundaries, to a symbiotic identification with the love of the subject, not leaving room for any independent action of the spirit. Thus live so called lower beings (lower?) – a dog dies of longing when his beloved master dies. People though, so called higher beings (higher?) are not prepared to resign to this extent from their internal independence. They always leave an empty space through which they glance at their objects of longing – nostalgically.

This is a two-fold determination, on the one hand un-obtainability and un-definitivity of the true subject of human longing, and on the other, a continual rejection of communion with him that threatens a loss of self and confronts us with a great empty place, which somehow needs to be filled. And this place is called time.

Professor Kępiński, a psychiatrist, in writing of time in melancholy, differentiates two means of stretching time. In the first, time lengthens, an instant becomes eternity. In the second, time dissolves in a mist, is without meaning, for nothing happens. In the first, one is a companion of eternity, in the second, a companion of nothingness. One way or another, in awaiting fulfilment that shall never come, something has to be done with that void.

One means of filling the void are rituals. Melancholies fill themselves with daily, ritual actions that provide the feeling that something occurs – one after the other. Sloterdijk calls it modern cynicism. That in nothingness there is, however, a variety of events that though not possessing this complete importance, are as a consequence familiar and easy to grasp.

The daily ritual of brewing tea at breakfast, which allows to sense the warmth bubbling in the kettle of water there, where human warmth is needed. The ritual of tying a tie in front of the mirror, with a careful look where the Adams Apple is – which never allows itself to be shaved precisely. The ritual of smoking a cigarette, motions of the hand, motions of the mouth and small objects present where they are expected.

The ritual of bodily love, suggestive motions of the hips and head, sequence of gestures that give short-term sense of fulfilment – quickly fading, forcing to pass on to other rituals such as lighting a cigarette, exchange of views...

The rituals of old-age, such as visits to the doctor, seeing children and grandchildren, meeting up with former comrades-at-arms, visiting friends at the cemetery that have passed away... The rituals of youth, wagging, weekend parties and alcohol, barracking for the team and the relief of matriculation. Playing chess. Also a ritual. Playing races. Playing Roulette. Playing the stock market. Various types of games, also psychological. Politics. The ritual of speaking. Speaking a series of sounds – words and sentences – and listening carefully to other such series that come from the outside.

And so we are helpless in the face of time, an entire ocean we need to fill.

On cruelty

Mr P.'s neighbour is kicking the dog on the balcony. Howling. Someone from the upper floor shouts into the dark:
'F...! Stop it!
A neighbourly mumble. He stops. Quiet.

Gratuitous cruelty. "A person harasses another without reason, only because it gives him joy", notes the writer Ryszard Kapuścinski. Why – without reason?! For harassment gives him joy! Can there be a better, more powerful motive to do anything at all? More powerful than experiencing the feeling of joy?

Why is cruelty a form of joy? Fromm's reply: The tormentor becomes drunk on their own power, own might – and grows, when subsumes the tormented. Is it possible to have a greater power over another being? Inflict pain and watch how they submit to it?

And what can the tormented do when they do not wish to bear it? They can die. But they do not die – meaning that they agree to the pain. They agree and therefore take part. A communion of tormentor and tormented. I torment you and you agree. Thugs do not like victims that die. They feel rejected by them.

A communion of tormentor and tormented. Better this than none. Man is a herd animal – if he cannot be loved, he seeks other human emotions. But do fear and hatred also form the picture? If they hate me, then at least they notice me. This means that I am. And it is not that difficult to evoke hatred. It's enough to have courage.

Enter the mind of the torturer. A dream: A dark cellar. Tied to a metal table. The last interrogators have left. They now know all. Only a sad, dull thug in a leather apron remains. Skin pale, eyes motionless. He chooses the players. You are all his. He looks at your fingers. Smiles. Finally he has someone, for himself only. Never before but now he has. It will hurt. Closeness hurts.

Emptiness and loneliness also hurts. Though somewhat other.

Fromm says, that individuals whose sense of independence is weak, who have to compensate their low sense of self-worth, attempt to gain it through domination – the one accessible form of closeness. What individuals does he have in mind? After all, we are all in the same boat. Only each to their own.

Because kicking in the face and similar behaviour leave numerous traces, being subject to possible criminal proceedings, in a liberal society only the short-sighted and unhinged resort to fisticuffs. There are many ways, without even touching someone with a finger, to throw them into the shredder. And to boot, declare that it's for their good. An example?

One can also cause pain by leaving someone in a void. For a void too is painful. It is sufficient to forget about this someone. Sufficient to look the other way, when they speak. Sufficient to take their own self. First to give, then to take, give and not give. Like heroin to a drug addict. Let them suffer. *They love me, even when they suffer.* A specialty of women. *Do they still love me, when I am not good?* Specialty of good girls.

Fromm: Cruelty is not normal. Tell us another – well it is. Though unpleasant. So as not to see how normal it is, we call it by another name. At times cruelty is known as mercy, sometimes concern for a moral spine. At times it appears in words such as 'Oh God, I forgot...' At times 'How can you be so.....?!'

Cruelty out of indifference. Someone forgets about the child – that shut itself in the wardrobe so that they worry. At least a bit. So that they search. So that in the end they find Johnny. One hour passes. A second – it is difficult to breathe. No one is searching. Time to leave the wardrobe. Home is quiet and empty. The child does not cry – there is no audience.

Cruelty by accident. Closed trains full of people for whom someone forgot to prepare water. Lack of organisational skills. No problem. They'll die anyway, any minute now.

The dog whimpers on the balcony. The neighbour sleeps alone. Again his wife did not return for the night.

On the sense of guilt

Either, or... Either one is guilty – and this signifies something appalling – a thing one cannot agree with for it leads to self contradiction. Or someone else is guilty, you, he, they... And all it takes is to find the guilty. *Tertium non datur.* That is why the sense of guilt looks around with the eyes of a wolf and looks to see who could be the victim for its fangs.

The wolf eyes of guilt are in addition mad. For the state of guilt, a state in which it is necessary to curse oneself, is unbearable. So unbearable that withstanding it demands a continual tightwire act of determining who, where, why could be more guilty and who will the fangs be able to sink into, and force that person to bear the terrified, empty look around them.

Who then let this beast out?

As with all beasts, as the feeling of guilt, it is easiest to blame the Creator. He created the world in which man from time to time commits evil – lying, betraying, murdering – and then placed a monster in him who hunts the wrongdoer. And lives on his life. Like a vampire. Maybe vampires exist for this reason? The ancient Greeks multiplied this monster and gave it the name of Erynie. Though everything there was simpler. For man in principle was not guilty. Erynie were the sign of the Gods' revenge, not guilt. Seemingly alike in construction, but not completely, for they differ.

Thus a world that is a trap for people. The Erynie hunt those that have fallen into this trap. No one could have not fallen in, could have stopped short of life. A mouse too, does not have to be tempted by the cheese, under which there lies a razor blade. If it lives though, it has no choice. For it is meant to eat that piece of cheese. It is so with man, for whom await the Erynie. He shall enter the world, kill his father, desecrate his mother and then they shall fly away and shall hunt him. For the revenge of the gods.

And the fangs of feeling guilt sink themselves into those who of their own will have committed evil. Not because they have had to. The Creator has added into this entire matter the issue of freedom of will, suggesting in this way that no one can blame him, the Creator. If the hot breath of feeling guilty is scorching you, if you are coated in perspiration out of fear of its huge fangs, it is only yourself that you have to blame.

The Creator knew full well that it is either.., or. And that the inevitable gaze of madness, wolf-like look of feeling guilt, shall be directed at him – the Creator himself. Therefore, in foresight He placed between Himself and man a wedge of free will. Into all manner of blame, all desire to transplace guilt, one predatory jump directed towards Providence.

A manoeuvre only partially effective. As it is, many a person raises their fist at the heavens.

Where though, has the trap gone, set for man – if no longer neither the world nor all the more, the Creator himself can be seen as a ruse? Well, man is a trap unto himself. Man falls into these wedges – those of his own life – the jaws of his deeds clamp down and then he casts about angrily with a wolf-like look, struggles, throws himself about and foams at the mouth.

And all in vain. Though perhaps not entirely. At times when he has someone close at his side – wife, mother or child – his fangs shall strike and cause such a pain that at least for a while someone else shall writhe in agony before him. And for a moment he shall forget about the clamping jaws of feeling guilty.

There is one means to free oneself. A wolf that falls into a trap can bite off its trapped limb – leave it in the jaws of the snare and move on. It is rare that man can muster the will to do this. And out of those that survive this torture, few survive.

Tear oneself away, leave a piece behind in your teeth – feeling of guilt – and live on. A narrative for man that is almost impossible. That is why usually the jaws inevitably crush us, their strength greater with every passing day lived, every new deed, compromise, wrongdoing, forgetting that they already are and will always be. And nothing can annul them, change, for the irreversibility of time's flow amounts to their power. Everything that has already been and that shall never not be, everything that one regrets and about which it can be said: *my God, if I had only known then, if I had done it another way, if I could do it once more.....*

And perhaps it is only this that one could be upset with the Creator. Why is it that everything can be experienced once, only once – that every moment is one and there is no return. That all the wrong gestures and looks will always now be to the end of the world – such as they were then, in that one moment, in which they arose. So as to form a burden on our backs? So as to grit our teeth and crush in the feeling of guilt – until madness comes, until we completely lose our way?

Is that really what it was all about?

On sorrow

Sorrow is alive. This is the greatest difference from feelings such as melancholy and depression, as well as despair. These emotional states are characterised by a halt to internal motion, identified as a void. Sorrow is akin to something that sails. In fact sorrow sails through those that experience it.

It is no accident therefore that art when it wishes to speak of sorrow very often turns to images that have something in common with a 'running' element. For example rain. A person sits by a window and gazes out at the street drenched in torrents of rain. The drumming of falling water, light of a rain-struck day, umbrellas and windows onto which raindrops splatter and passersby hurdling puddles...

In Andriej Tarkovski's films sorrow is an enduring state, one very clearly present. It is present not so much in accounts of people's lives (though by no means absent there) as – in a mysterious way – in the images of things, the state of things and time. Mr P. remembers one such image: the tiled floor of some abandoned hospital or baths, observed from 50 or 60 centimetres above. The gaze follows the once white, broken tiles where one sees every now and then old, worn out objects such as spectacles with a broken lens, a needle, yellowed photographs...

Does this suffice to fix an image of sorrow?

Well no – this is not sorrow yet. Too much anxiety here. Anxiety and fear have nothing in common with sorrow – they after all feed on hope dying.

In Tarkovski's film the floor is swept over by water. All the objects that the camera stops at are under a transparent sheet of water. Material at every moment where some thing is brought into view is a wave, motion of water. And separation. Water has already taken these objects from our world, changed their meaning, carried them and though they are motionless, they sail ever further away.

This is sorrow. Becoming distant from what is completed. The fact that something is now 'on the other side', there where it now cannot have such meaning or rationale, as it had 'here'. Beyond reach and seemingly still present. The sheet of water, a windowpane where former photographs bear witness to this condition.

The first weeks and months after every separation, regardless whether caused by death or simply departure is in fact a life among the symptoms of presence fading away. An empty, unused ashtray, clothes that demand to be thrown into the washing machine, a cup into which one would like to pour tea.

Existence in this state is a continual halting of awareness, a braking of its tendency to stitch every object with some scenario taken from memory.

Thoughts though run along a well worn path and not realising that the world had changed irreversibly, fall into a trap of objects that had lost meaning. This strange form of motion is in fact sorrow. Tears welling in one's eyes when things no one needs any more spin around.

In the stream of sorrow in which one is allowed to flow, the world before begins to distance itself. Sobbing, crying and sometimes simply a deep sigh, allow to place the seal of departure with something that now simply is no more. Allow that period to find closure. An empty ashtray no longer is filled by the image of fingers holding a cigarette. This image was washed away from awareness by a cascade of flowing sorrow – one certain day to forget sorrow too, the ashtray is thrown into the rubbish and then the spirit opens towards a new presence.

Worse, when awareness diligently avoids falling into the stream of sorrow. When it circles on the edge of recollections, examines them but does not agree on falling into the depths that accompany forgetting. The past then never recedes. The dam that halts sorrow is built continually anew with situations recycled, words from 'why', sentences that in truth express a lack of agreement, one for the fact that the ashtray is no longer needed.

On fear

Fear is a gobbler of the spirit. But what in fact does fear gobble? Surely not the immortal spirit? The immortal spirit belongs to the order of things where there is no place for gobbling. There is yet another matter.

The word fear evokes the thought of rats. A grey wave of oncoming rodents, a vibrating, shapeless mass of blurred outlines under which something is hidden. In this image, darkness, greyness plays an important role. Fear is grey, fear blurs the image, removes the various colours and varieties from the world, hides its real meaning. Fear turns everything into one dimension, a dimension of danger.

When evening, at the bus stop, Mr P. asks an elderly woman for the time and she jumps, backing off, looking at him as if she were a rabbit, he feels as if a transformation has occurred. Together with all the world he is the face of a wolf. A world of wolf faces. When a man loses the woman he loves – in turn apologising and beating her – and when drunk goes to her for he wishes to embrace her, he already has the face of a wolf. She then cries out.

A person in fear is absolutely alone. All around there is a homogenous, grey crowd of wolf faces and a person alone. A person in fear cannot trust anyone, only attack and run. A person in fear cannot recognise a gesture such as the friendship of an outreached hand – for them the hand is an instrument of danger. A person in fear never hears the merry sound of laughter coming from somewhere. It is the wolves that laugh at his expense. They are cut off from the world, alone and are other. Never trusting anyone.

The opposite of fear is not courage. The opposite of fear is trust. Fear eats into trust, trust as a bond to the other, belonging to the other, and to the common world here and now. How does it come to the breaking of this bond?

Kępiński, the psychiatrist, describes such an imagined situation. I hear the door bell. I open and see someone with the face of a wolf. I am afraid – just then the other raises their hand and takes off the wolf mask. The smiling face of a friend appears. I sense relief – everything in the world has returned to its place. Then the other raises their hand and takes off the mask of friend. Again the snout of a wolf appears.

Kępiński calls this type of fear terror. It is based on a complete destruction of trust towards the world. The world does not meet any expectations – every subsequent situation is a negation of the internal order that man has shaped within. There, where a person expects a face, a snout appears. When they wish to battle with the snout – a friend appears. Could kill the friend. Remain alone. But they are not alone. Wishes to embrace the friend regained. Raise their eyes and confront the snout. The person becomes motionless. The world is seemingly an endless snout. And there is nothing else. This is terror.

A person bound in terror becomes motionless. But not a person in fear. They attack or run. Why so? Defend from threats. What do they defend? When we began to consider fear, the image of rats appeared, an image flowing along some grey mass. This hidden 'something' is very important. It still exists, though it is now completely unseen. Engulfed through fear, it in fact gives it meaning – fear devours it up to the moment that it exists. They, who have lost it completely, no longer feel fear. Maybe terror. Though now they cannot feel nothing. They do not need to battle, to flee. They are 'Muselmen'.

In fact this is the spirit, this devoured 'something'.

The 20th century was awash in fear. In contrast the 19th century was a time of hope. Hope and faith in progress, in the so called victory of reason, in the emancipation of man. Emancipation was to eventuate through the development of science or also through revolution. There is a direct connection between the hope of the 19th century and the danger of the 20th . He who is afraid is the one who loses hope. He who has, loses.

The inquisition also created fear. And not by coincidence. Faith creates huge hope and enormous ties between those that believe. As faith in salvation and eternal life during the Middle Ages. The faithful were those who unconditionally trusted each other, trusted also the world that was meant to come. In the poverty and starvation of every day they lived in their world of faith and community of belief. Until one day the friend up to now – one who was most trusted – appeared and had the snout of a wolf. Suddenly it transpired that there is no world of faith and salvation – there is only poverty and loneliness in the face of a wolf snout. This was fear. Or even terror. Yes, rather terror.

Ordinary fear appeared though earlier, before man was dragged out of home. Not so much those arrested who experienced fear as those waiting to be arrested. Those who experience fear are those who are still waiting to lose work. Those who experience fear are those already thrown out of work but still have money and the right to the dole. Or those who in their pocket harbour the last scrap of paper with the address of someone who promises employment. Fear lives on dying hope. Fear is the waiting.

Man walks among people, passes smiling faces on the street, looks friends into their eye. But already knows. Under these masks lies in wait the snout of a wolf. Fear eats into the human spirit. Man waits.

On anxiety

According to the clinical definition, fear is different from anxiety in that it always refers to something concrete, some defined danger, whilst the latter refers to something that we are unable to pinpoint. Anxiety has no subject per se.

Inspite of the seeming clarity as well as great utility, this definition has important weaknesses, it is possible to say – as is often with definitions – more questions arise than answers. The main problem is as follows. If anxiety has no subject, then how do we know that we are in fact experiencing it? After all, in order to make ourselves aware, we need to present something as such. This has to be the subject of our consciousness, has to somehow appear so as to be grasped.

And in what way does anxiety appear? Well – by definition – it does not, at all. For if it did appear, we would have a phenomenon of sorts, some object of consciousness. Anxiety though is so intimate, so tied to the core of our existence that it cannot exist in this sphere of objectivity that is the sphere of cognition. Anxiety is the nothingness in our very selves.

The above reasoning could be criticised for the fact that it does not entirely base on the definition given earlier. For after all, the point is not the complete inability to be aware of one's anxiety but that being apprehensive we are afraid but do not know why. But what does it mean that we do not know that we are afraid? In what way do we learn of our emotional state? This in general is a very difficult issue.

Bergson noted – and it would appear that no one has thought of anything better – that emotional states reach us 'colouring' as if various phenomena that are specific to them, though at the same time not revealing themselves, not taking up any fragment of our psychological space. This in fact is the case with fear. We come to realise when we see something terrible. As it was said, a wolf snout awakens fear. It is terrible.

And when there is no snout? Or anything else that could be terrible apart from the state we are in? Here in fact we come closer to anxiety. Though only closer. The very fact of becoming aware of this condition in which we are and defining it as anxiety signifies that in objectifying it, changing from a situation when we are afraid without an awareness of trepidation, to a situation in which trepidation is identified and through its place in language, somehow domesticated. Thus naming anxiety in fact changes it into fear. A means of dealing with anxiety.

We therefore have a situation in which anxiety, the subject of our discussion, is in fact inaccessible. We need to continually bear this in mind, otherwise there is the danger of a simple mistake whereby we shall treat the structure raised in discussion as the framework of anxiety. That is not the case. Whatever is said of anxiety, regardless of its label, we shall always have to deal not so much with it as our own attempts at grasping it – how we come to deal with anxiety. Anxiety is hidden, open are a great range of phenomena and actions that take its place.

It can be said that property of anxiety – that it is an 'empty place' in various chains of events and thoughts – deserves close attention. We have therefore here a mechanism creating irrationality. A 'machine' thanks to which a rational person suddenly becomes irrational. An irrationality that surprises this person, however, one that must be accepted as fact. A sudden superstition, unexplainable outbursts of anger, excessive attention to how the stomach and heart work, insomnia where tomorrow becomes a sentence to be served...

There is always a lack of a previous link, some bridge that would join these curious, irrational phenomena into a whole – how a person feels, their personality, character, identity. The sequence of causes and results remains broken, but only seemingly. The mechanism has functioned – there where an unseen abyss of anxiety should appear, strange, incomprehensible entities have surfaced. Consciousness though is susceptible, it would appear to it that suddenly out of nothing in particular, in an empty room where music could be heard, an irrational vision took hold; a car accident that killed close ones, cells that are now cancer, murderers about to strike the house. Here in fact the empty link of anxiety is filled. It is a bridge that is missing – in its place images awakening fear have taken their place.

What happens though when we attempt to leave from a bordering territory, where what we know of anxiety results from replacing anxiety with fear? When do we throw overboard all fear by saying that where it appears, anxiety is no longer there? Let us take a good look at the world in the unseen light of anxiety. It shall be different, of a different shape and it is this that allows to see in fact anxiety.

***

In this world we shall not be afraid of anything. Thus in contrast to fear, which colours phenomena associated into one concrete, defined means – anxiety first of all deforms. Or perhaps to put in another way, anxiety does not so much as deform phenomena as such but destroys the above described means of relations between them, the space in which they come to be. It twists and jumbles it like an old canvas until in the end, things stripped of their fundamental essence deform, fall onto one another and mix in an incomprehensible and chaotic way. But a conscious fear does not accompany this, for there where there is fear, anxiety is no more.

A person experiencing anxiety therefore lives with a deformed world, one that is strange and sad. Roads in this world do not lead anywhere for after all the groundwork of meanings – one that endows every journey with meaning – has disintegrated like a well trodden rag. The hills that are climbed multiply into infinity, and from each the view is the same. In the world of anxiety time is a lifeless snail, falls into some abyss or stops suddenly, unable to find a way in the disintegrating space of meanings. It is paralysed for it lacks an essential continuum and this in fact is warped by anxiety. Memory in the world of anxiety is also affected by the lack of groundwork – and to fill this loss there repeat into infinity some chance images, fragments of talks, sentences overheard in dead-end streets. In the light of anxiety the person vanishing observes a vanishing world.

We need to remember though that a person does not know they are in the throes of anxiety. They see only – and the vision is appalling – the world is escaping them and disintegrating, nothing belongs to anything – they are increasingly isolated and cannot see this. As Georg Samsa discovers, in contrast to all other people he heard of or knew, he has an insect claw with hooks, lies in mouldy bed linen on his wing-sheath back, is alone and there is little chance that someone shall help him turn over on to the right side.

In such a state a person cannot remain long. This is unbearable. They have to do something, something that allows to find some basis of reality. One that ties the fragments escaping of things, giving them back a name and place. Foremost revealing and establishing in the world the source of the unseen ray of anxiety, one that deforms everything. If that is not done, every attempt, every move shall deepen the disintegration, isolation and alienation. As in the struggle of a great cockroach, one that Samsa became. If that is not done, then in the end they shall lie like stone, a cast wax figure with staring eyes fixed in a void falling like a deck of cards, head cocked away from the pillow. In a condition known as catatonia. Then they shall perish.

Usually though, a person in a state of anxiety attempts to free themselves of this unbearable condition. This attempt is always some sort of activity. Intellectual or physical. If the physical precedes the intellectual then – because anxiety has no subject – it becomes totally senseless and appears as an attack of rage.

Usually though, activity is focused first on giving the unbearable some objective meaning, understanding its causes and through understanding – marking out a means of action that can remove the unbearable. It is necessary therefore to put together the bits and pieces of a disintegrating world. The means of linking all that is escaping shall be called interpretation. Wandering along the offices, Joseph K. searches for an interpretation of his unbearable – process.

Interpretation is every operation that allows to move the source of anxiety from the sphere of the unseen into the graspable, find the source in the world of objects, define its boundaries and spin a web of cause-result dependencies that even if peculiar, change a subject-less anxiety into a fear of something that is named. According to Hannah Arendt and – surprisingly on her side – Jacques Lacan, in our understanding, interpretation therefore plays a role that is attributed to the metaphorical structure of human language. Most of all, however, interpretation makes possible the removal of anxiety from the most intimate, internal sphere of the I, moving it into the external where anxiety no longer destroys the core of being. Interpretation rescues existence.

***

The instrument that allows to fill the most intimate nothingness cannot come from this nothingness. Therefore the instrument of interpretation has to tie itself to the world of phenomena, with the world of others. And let us not be confused into misunderstanding; very often someone puts forward an interpretation at a moment they are alone. The point is not though the physical non-presence of the other (though that too has its meaning in the choice of interpretation instrument) but the fact that the interpretation has to come from without. From traditions and culture, or – to say it another way – a linguistic identification of sensory experience.

But always from without. Therefore in anxiety the Other is essential. Dealing with anxiety amounts to always grasping someone else who throws a lifeline of interpretation. At the same time though because in anxiety the structure of the world is disintegrating, a person avoids everything that may destabilise it further. And in fact allowing the Other into my inner space amounts to always disturbing the groundwork of my world. Therefore finding interpretation is in anxiety akin to balancing on a line between an attempt to maintain an impossible coherence of the world and closing its boundaries – a rescue thanks to the help of the Other, thanks to the opening of boundaries.

That is why the need of the present Other can take on a great range of surprising forms. This variety is already easier to identify and describe. We therefore return to the borderlands, an area where usually what is called anxiety is in fact a means of coping with anxiety. And its transformation into a personal, bewildering fear smattered with a sprinkling of horror.

One of the most simple, most basic means of objectifying anxiety is placing it in 'the liver'. This means searching for the source of anxiety in various bodily illnesses. The strength of a hypochondriac's interpretation lies no doubt in the fact that the body is relatively closest to the I. Some thinkers identify it even one with the other. And at the same time is mercilessly concrete, objective and in fact, palpable.

Anxiety brings forth powerful stimuli and paths of imagination – a distended stomach, painful kidney, pins in the heart that can explain the general state of disintegration and discouragement that the I packs the world with. In addition these feelings and images are so primal that they do not require the strong participation of the Other and their refined instruments of interpretation. They allow the subject of interpretation to maintain alienation and autonomy and at the same time, build anew a rational world. Several words that the child learns to use when they are three, allows to express the entire web of unpleasantness and trepidation.

Eternally returning in the complaints of hypochondriacs: 'it was most likely something not fresh...' or 'I've got pins here, in my heart...', can be a key to understanding a person rotting in the anxiety of the internal world. And when a person in anxiety then discovers this means of interpretation they can always find someone who will eagerly listen and propose a cure – doctor, neighbour or finally some other type of healer.

Not all though in a state of anxiety reach for a hypochondriacal interpretation. In a severe case of anxiety – and we ought to remember we are speaking of an abyss, nothingness, of something that is never experienced directly – there often appears an interpretation that entangles the entire available world in the construction of a sense of danger.

Everyone is evil, lurking in waiting for a person suffering anxiety, wishing to destroy them, rob, murder and so as to achieve this they communicate through secret knocks, leaving everywhere hidden signs and organise themselves and link – only they are the victim of this conspiracy. Understanding this, the person feels relief in a way, ceases therefore to dwell in an unbearable void. And undertakes a feverish activity. A madness of activity.

***

Why therefore is it that some find the missing link of fear in their stomach and others, in the harmful actions of their social brethren?

Searching for the mask of anxiety in this or other area of reality is already the effect of a deeper choice, a choice imposed by an intersection of factors deciding on the means of identity being construed. They in fact determine what comes to fill the space of the I. And foremost, whether the fundament of identity becomes the 'external'. Thus ties with others, belonging and responsibility to others, or also the 'internal' – my organs, experience tied to them, their needs and finally the autonomic I. The road of life, boundary separating me from others.

As we suspect, in traditional societies individual identity is constituted foremost on the basis of external relations – belonging to a chain of generations, social roles played out in relation to others, mythical 'in common' blood of the dynasty. Whilst in cultures built around monotheistic religions, relations are built with God. And when we say 'identity is constructed...', we have in mind the deepest possible meaning. As if to say that a person really experiences their own self as a part, one that belongs, tied to something greater. That always, when the thought comes or emotions do that relate personally, then as a matter of necessity they relate also to others – for their I, their identity, crystallizes somewhere on the line between their own person and others.

For such a person a subject-less anxiety that is only just searching for an interpretation is in principle impossible. Such a person in their very core, there where anxiety appears as nothingness, is already defined to a strong interpretation. In its core there is God or gods, in its core there is conscience, forebears and relatives. Anxiety becomes immediately a responsibility or a sense of guilt.

***

Modernitas has robbed us of this comfort. Variability and change have swept all that is univocal. For a while still it appeared that the source of interpretation could be the process of change itself – though as we all know – utopias built on this concept have come crashing down with a loud clang. Identity ceased to be an obvious position in the world, became a problem. People who of themselves are travellers as Zygmunt Bauman says, nomads of their own choice or not, people whose world in the course of one life changes many times and so as to exist they have to foremost, define boundaries – this is I, this is not I. And when nothing beyond the boundary of the I is permanent, the tendency becomes natural for everything that is the most important in the world, where the core of existence can be found – to be positioned and seen in their own selves. And thus there arises a huge, empty area, a cosmos of the I that needs to be filled.

It is no coincidence therefore that together with *modernitas* there has been a huge growth of thinking, which sets itself the aim of understanding and interpretation of the I distended like a balloon. This empty area was filled with various theories, egology theoretical and applied, numerous hermeneutics that allow the naming of a living nothingness of the spirit. And together with these the art of speaking about anxiety has become widespread.

The worst off are those who are stripped of the opportunity to belong to the world of tradition, not having integrated into the thick of postmodern interpretations. A person whose interior without boundaries does not find either fear of God – for God has forsaken them – or dread of people – for they can forsake people of their own accord. And reflecting upon the condition of their own viscera is considered lacking in elegance, whilst the looking glass offered by the professional interpreter of the *psyche*, awakens an enormous resistance. These very people long for something that is beyond their own selves but they lack words to name this – and besides they do not believe in the sense of doing so. Only an extended insomnia is left, filled by a feverish rush of thoughts – yesterday's failures, tomorrow's problems. All in the unseen glare of anxiety.

On envy

The lips shaped, twisted in an envious smile is very characteristic. It is not though always recognised. A smile itself is a sign that lulls watchfullness. Normally we react to a smile with trust – for it is deeply encoded in our nature. So when someone smiles to us beautifully, we stop looking in their face for any sign of trouble. Though if we were to look more closely....

It is easier to carefully follow the lips that do not smile to us. This is possible when a group of people gathers, one forced into an exchange of smiles among which some are smiles of envy. For example during a *party*.

A beautiful woman greets her friend. Both are elegantly dressed, hair groomed with the utmost of care – one has hers gathered in a clip at the back and that is why her face is clearly seen. They exchange smiles, lean forward; a delicate brush of mutual cheeks allows avoiding any traces of scarlet lipstick on the cheek. Their glances are set in the distance.

The fact that a smile is one of envy is most clearly signalled by the expression of the eyes. They are cold, filled with hatred and watchful. They betray. That is why seasoned players when smiling in envy do not show their eyes. So as to hide them they resort to two strategies. The first is to look into the distance and that is what our two female friends do. An elegant strategy but without emotion. The second is based on covering the eyes, eyelids drawn. This can be done by winking – then the emitted signal suggests: I am merry and sympathetic, smile from ear to ear and that is why I blinked. Or closing one's eyelids calmly, as if falling asleep – an expression of trust as if saying: I am all yours, coming closer and not controlling you with my eyes.

And under the eyelids, hidden ice.

Though even if the eyes' expression is carefully masked over, the lips betray envy. This arises because anger, an integral element of envy forces the corners of the mouth to move to the side. This is all about a threatening, atavistic demonstration of the teeth. And as if the whole face did not try to be part of a radiating smile, the corners shall wander down to the side. This means that the lips of envy have a somewhat wave-like shape and in addition the furrow on the cheek disappears, one part of the smile. Naturally this also can be masked. Women use lipstick for this purpose. Highlighting their lower lip, they change the expression of anger into a cocktail of blush and pride, which is rather alluring – especially for men.

If the means of masking over anger is a smile, then the stiffening of the corner is almost unseen. Then, however, an expression appears typical for envy – a pale smile and fleeing or blinking eyes. Somewhat as if someone chewed in fact something tart or bitter. Envy has a bitter taste. It is bitter in the bitterness of tar added to honey. It is as bitter as bitterness whose taste one wishes to hide.

For envy is one of the feelings most commonly masked. It is easier to admit – to oneself and others – to similar feelings of jealousy. But not to envy. Envy thus, being a feeling that is clearly antagonistic to those close, mercilessly reveals the weakness of those who experience it. And there is nothing more shameful than weakness. And no one shall show concern for someone filled with envy.

Envy is as if the embryo of the relationship that is jealousy and hatred. How is it different from jealousy? The jealous, when seeing the neighbour in a great big car think to themselves: *Why is it that I don't have one of those? I have to get a loan at once and buy myself one that is even bigger.* The envious though think: *How did that son of a bitch get enough money to buy one of those? I hope he crashes it, his wife betrays him, and that he gets cancer...*

In fact jealousy is a very constructive feeling, thanks to which exemplary husbands are an example to all at work and exemplary wives scrub and polish pots and kitchen floor to a gleaming mirror. Envy though, is an emotion of the weak. A feeling of those hit hardest by fate, those that have lost out, those who never manage a loan from the bank, for at the sight of them, bankers sense a mixture of distrust and pity. Then shut their safe with a firm thud.

Thus they only have hatred left. But hatred also demands strength. So as to give vent to hatred, courage is needed. This the envious lacks – how could they be courageous when they consider themselves a nobody? Thus a resort to magic: in their imagination some force destroys those that are better, stronger, bigger than they. Raping their wife, taking their savings – making them weak and helpless, such as they are. Because life has consistently taught the envious they will never be more than human waste, in their mind they turn others into human waste. This meets the intuitive need for a sense of equality.

Envy functions in the social fabric like a spider's venom on an insect's body. It does not destroy it – as of course would hatred – but deprives it of substance. People seen through the prism of envy cease being human, the entire complex architecture of their mutual relations vanishes. They become empty shells, imprisoned in the spider web of ignominy that encases them.

Max Scheler pointed out that envy does not flourish in societies where human inequality is sanctioned by religion and customs as in Hindu cast society but in those where – similar to European societies – a relative equality of rights goes hand in hand with an enormous disproportion in factual power, possession, education – where "everyone has the right to be equal with everyone and despite this in reality cannot be equal".

Therefore, Mr. P. thinks, surely two generations shall pass, everyone shall be a great deal more wealthy and the old joke about the Polish cauldron in hell where devils are not needed shall still be relevant. For when someone tries to leave, the remainder will drag them back in.

On disquiet

Disquiet is a difficult state of emotion to grasp. It differs in terms of genre from love, anger or joy – emotions that wash over in a great wave, oceanic – of distinct hues and light. Disquiet differs even from impatience, yet is an integral part of its family. Not so complete, anticipated but taking up little space, hidden in darkness or darkness itself. Nonetheless – as every emotion – in its own way painting all that is found in us. Disquiet that irritates. An untreated tooth. A broken fingernail. A sentence unsaid.

In The Eight Octavo Notebooks Franz Kafka wrote: "There are two main human sins from which all the others derive: impatience and indolence. It was because of impatience that they were expelled from Paradise, it is because of indolence that they do not return. Yet perhaps there is only one major sin: impatience. Because of impatience they were expelled, because of impatience they do not return."[3] (The Third Octavo Notebook, 1991:87)

In Paradise man impatiently reached out for an apple. This was the first sin. Though it can be said that the essence of the second sin was not so much impatience but disquiet. A sign of which is the kinship with sloth proposed by Kafka.

A scene typical of disquiet. A man in a white suit sits at a cafe table. The table is small, round, on the footpath outside. An empty small coffee cup. The man is thin, his face a grimace. Tapping the table with his cigarette case. Delicately, quietly. Is there anyone else there apart from him?

Here we come to the particular traits of disquiet, making it distinct from impatience. From the point of view of the first it is all the same whether the man is alone or not. Let us accept that apart from the man there is no one else at the table. It can be assumed that he is impatient because he is waiting for someone. This is the simplest scenario. The man is irritated because the place where the other person should be is empty. Should be – therefore no doubt they had arranged to be, and he or she is running late. From an analyst's point of view the case is clear. The other person comes, then the man stops being impatient. He shall erupt in anger, shout and gesticulate – or smile helplessly. One way or another, will set sail for other oceans in the weather of the spirit.

We return to the table. Another person sits there. A brunette in a summer dress. Just arrived. Engrossed in the mirror, correcting her make-up. And the man? His eyes are not fixed on her but around her, somewhat to her side. His face a grimace. Tapping with his cigarette case. He is anxious. Perhaps because she is engrossed in the mirror. She lifts her gaze, looks at him in anticipation. He

---

3   Franz Kafka *The Blue Octavo Notebooks*, ed Max Brod, translated by Ernst Kaiser & Eithne Wilkins, Exact Change.

says something quietly – we can guess it's not pleasant. The grimace on his face has not changed at all. Her presence has not changed anything.

Disquiet is very much different from impatience. One can become impatient for a particular reason. Such as for instance someone's tardiness when we have arranged to meet. When the reason goes, impatience is cured. Disquiet though is a different matter. It does not relate to anything that can be grasped and continues regardless of changes in our immediate environment. Of a similar ilk is the family of moods such as anxiety, boredom or nostalgia – emotions without a defined subject. This: "draws back and forth like silent fog in the abysses of Dasein",[4] Heidegger claims (1995:78).

Though disquiet is related to these, it is not synonymous. It has no concrete, directly graspable cause but at the same time is identified with a restless waiting, with a depressing feeling that at any moment something will occur, something must happen now. In disquiet this feeling of immediate relations with fulfilment is fundamental. A continual oscillation between the conviction that one is only a step away and disappointment, loss in a typical way makes for an askew expression of impatience's grimace.

This internal entrapment lies at the heart of the inability to take action, typical for those who lack quietude. Thus the hesitation of Kafka when contemplating the nature of the second sin. He knows that sloth is the key but also that it is not self sufficient – arising from disquiet.

If our man in question has made at least one sensible move calculated to change his situation, this would have meant that he accepted the imperfect, incomplete means of existence – that is the source of his irritation – and decided of his own to correct and better it. In this fashion he would have taken the responsibility unto himself but in fact does not wish to do so and cannot.

He does not wish to for he waits until finally the clear promise that is hidden, shall be kept – one which he comes to understand as the imperfection of everything that is around him. He knows that the world is a step away from this. And therefore also senses that not only does he not wish to, but also that he cannot, do anything. In doing something, anything, man would free of responsibility the one who had not finished the work and would have lost the opportunity for his return. He would have to struggle with ruined things on his own, wallowing in subsequent lack of fulfilling moments – burdened by the weight that after all, someone else should be carrying.

Those filled with disquiet do not accept the consequences of being banished from Paradise. They think it is a mistake, everything here is temporary and any

---

4   Martin Heidegger,*The Fundamental Concepts Of Metaphysics* translated by W. Mcneill and N. Walker, Indiana University Press.

moment someone will ferret in the files, realise the situation, make up for their mistake and make sure that matters take their proper course. Those bound in disquiet ought not to therefore take any action – not as before when impatient and on the instigation of the serpent and woman, man consumed the apple.

Tapping the cigarette case, face in a grimace, gazing into a void, the man in a white suit gives signs of his disquiet. In fact that is all he can do, and continue to repeat. The woman in the summer dress takes this personally, thinks that she is the source of this impatience. Is it because she was late? Corrects her make-up, smiles at him with a hint of invitation.

In fact though she senses that she cannot do a thing – that the man's disquiet is not her concern. 'That's just the way he is' – the words form in her head. The analyst could add that the worst in him is self deception. He is filled to the brim with lackness, which mistakenly believes that everything is there for the taking but all the same, will not make the move that is required to achieve this. In this refusal he wallows and waits, unchanged – with his grimace, cigarette case, tapping.

Let us accept that these hues of emotions define the climate of time. This entire scene somehow lends itself to the turn – of the 20th century. The age of disquiet ? A version of Triest, Sarajewo or Berlin. Men in white hats gazing into the void, beyond the heads of women. They sense that any moment a great change shall come. The impatience of *fin de siecle* wedges itself between the impatient abyss of the age of progress, and the deadly infatuation of the first days of The Great War.

On flattery

In drawing flatterers, whispering into the ear of the vain, Honoré Daumier curiously bends human figures. They turn heads to one another and at the same time are distant in a way that does not leave any doubt; this is a clash of antagonistic forces, ambiguous intentions. Daumier's drawings even when their titles do not contain even the slightest allusion to flattery, often are imbued with their own personal atmosphere of trivial, somewhat secretive talks. From the lips of flatterers whispers seep like honey, sweet, sticky, bringing to a standstill. Bringing the vain to a standstill. While the flatterer is immersed in feverish activity.

Flattery is one of the figures of inequality. Daumier, is its painter. That is why no doubt, over his grotesque twisted, disfigured characters turned to each other there wafts the scent of flattery. A lawyer, a lean and tall pettifogger turns to form a question mark so as to reach the ear of his abundantly girthed, now starch-like *vatermoerder* client. One actor with a blurred face, hand over his mouth, drips something to the other, whose mouth slowly stretches into a viper's smile. Daumier's line is able to capture the grotesque caricature that is testimony to the internal contradiction embedded in relation to flattery. Always that leaning towards, linked to a sense of distance, a withdrawal from the field of vision.

Withdrawal here plays a key part. The eyes of the vain subject, charmed by flattery, can never in truth see the figure of the beguiler. They must always turn towards some other object, towards someone beyond the immediate presence. Flattery is a triangle in which apart from the flatterer and the vain a third element is still necessary. This third element can be someone who is worse than the vain, duller or uglier, or something that is not worthy of them, or the whole world that is rolled out at their very feet. And he who rolls out this world is the flatterer.

This is the source of his dangerous power. Himself slipping by like a shadow, almost not present, an unnoticed voice, with his very breath practically throws the vain world to his feet, bending low, lighting fireworks. It is he who is the master of the imagination of his protagonist – the latter does not exist without him. His ego brought to life and stretched with the breath of the flatterer could disappear if this breath were to lack. Like a director, the flatterer is unseen but decides what transpires on the stage of emotions of the vain. This in fact is what makes flattery so tempting.

Aspersion, a close relative of flattery, allows the flatterer to gain one more profit. Equally effectively raising the vain when in words and imagination upon sinking some unfortunate whose baseness and abjection makes for a flatterrer's canvas, upon which the greatness and splendid worthiness of the 'flatteree' gleams like a diamond. At the same time though the flatterer can provide perhaps a sense of community with the vain, feed with his own – as previously mentioned – somewhat illusory person with the radiance of inflated greatness at the expense of the one sacrificed in blood, put down as it were, through aspersion. Himself as every sacrificer, feels though he is higher than the unfortunate put to the sword.

A successful process of flattery demands that the flatterer engages deeply into the situation of the triangle, where he is master of ceremonies conducted in honour of the vain. This demands, however, so as to – regardless of what in truth the flatterer thinks of his about to be charmed prey – see him for a moment in all his elevatedness, to quiver before his imagined majesty, which he himself is the creator. He has to mortify himself, bend low before someone, who at the very moment he himself surpasses.

That is why also language distinguishes as particularly bold – or in fact shameless – flattery pursued face to face. To beguile looking someone straight in the eyes is a singular ability. Snake-like, close to hypnosis. Demanding that the flatterer, in spite of the fact he is standing directly opposite the vain, become transparent to such a degree that instead of his own person there appears before the subject of charms, entirely different images, images of the subject's own elevatedness.

Although transparent, the flatterer has to concentrate all the attention all the time of the 'flatteree'. For even if for a moment he'd really disappear, the spell of flattery would have to burst. At the same time though, having the ordinary and to be quite frank rather plain semblance of the 'flatteree' before him, he has to maintain within this state of humiliation, one that allows to create words in a smokescreen of delusion. This is a source of venom and desire for revenge, one that always dwells in the spin of compliments. Sooner or earlier the vain shall be pushed into an abyss they allowed themselves to be led to so easily.

It is rare to find people who are resistant to the hypnotic charm of flattery. What is interesting, they are of two completely different tribes. The first are those who somewhere deep inside have an encoded conviction of their own ignominy, nothingness, hopeless lack of merit whatsoever. Naturally they constitute splendid material to become flatterers. Though flattery itself is no temptation, for they cannot believe even in the whitest of fibs – moreover, if someone tells even a positive truth, they won't believe it anyway.

The second are those who have enough calm in themselves that they do not need to hear paeans on their perfection. These find flattery strange in every exaggeration and puffed-upness and their somewhat childish view with difficulty breaks away from the present at the side of the flatterer. So as to travel in the footsteps of his words into the fictional world of I. Flattery thus always lives on insecurity, dreams of greatness, deluded hope all too easily falling into the abyss of bitterness. It lives on a shaky self image, sometimes flying skywards, other times wading in mud, in the image of a worm.

On respect or neo-cannibalism

Transplanting the organs of the deceased to those dying does not differ much from eating these organs as part of a ritual feast. Both in one and the other the point centres around strengthening the vital forces of the living at the expense of those who are not. There is, however, a certain difference between the 'operations' of cannibals and those of surgeons. And neither does it lie either in the purpose for which organs are taken, or in the manner of introducing them to the recipient's organism. This is not that important. The difference lies in the fact that cannibals usually (though not always) are responsible for the death of the donor. Surgeons on the other hand, though impatiently waiting for the latter's natural passing, usually at the same time maintain the life of the donor (about to pass), for medical ethics so require.

Thus contemporary society confronts doctors not so much with the dilemma of the cannibal – which life shall be taken so as to support another life – but rather to what extent the desecration of the dead is permissible for saving a life, or rather avoiding death. To what extent does saving before death release us from respect for the dead? How did we come to make a choice that allows us in the name of one value to totally disregard another? This conflict is the heart of the matter.

For many there is no conflict here, or this conflict is not important. The value of life exceeds the respect for the dead so much that there can be no discussion. After all, during autopsy the body is cut apart purely for diagnosis, so as to confirm or negate, cause of death. Life has value, all the more if a 'part' of the deceased can save another before death.

The problem begins when the donor organ has to be still 'warm', meaning it is necessary to remove it from a still 'partially living' person. Then the issue of the fine line between life and death rears its head. Thus, if it were possible to define precisely what this was... The real issue is that it isn't possible. In fact it would seem that dying is a continuous process, one stretched across time. Just as it would seem, the appearance of life itself. The inability of defining this second boundary when a new person appears, makes another conflict insoluble – the conflict about abortion.

The paradox of 'neo-cannibalism' together with the hidden issue of the boundary between life and death forces one to ask: why in fact are we to treat the dead with respect? Who are the dead that we owe them respect? Does a void, a non-life deserve anything at all?

For it would appear that on a day-to-day basis death is for us foremost a non-life, a loss in absence. How many times do parents in answer to a child's question about an uncle who has passed away, say he's gone away, not here.

The dead are not present in another way. They are simply not there. This is linked with what Philip Ariès describes as the non-presence of dying itself in our daily routine. We die in hospitals and our closest of kin know little of this. There is no bedside watch by the family and vigil later in the company of the body (together with children as in traditional cultures), it is not washed and dressed, given its final respects, often not even time itself is given. All these are taken care of by specialised workers. Who then are the dead for us? No one. They do not evoke respect. They evoke fear.

Let us repeat: the dead are not, as in traditional societies 'Someone other-present'. They disappear. And the body? What body? Easy to forget. And if several fragments of 'that something' can be useful to someone, save someone – then why not?

What does it mean to be 'other-present'? First of all, to be someone as such. This means that there exists a certain continuity between someone alive and dead. This continuity is difficult to comprehend from the perspective where the boundary between the existence of an individual and 'the rest of the world' is absolute and cannot be breached – from which in fact the only existence is 'my existence'. When it ends, everything becomes a non-life, nothing, no longer anything. The continuity between life and death can be grasped when one is able to see 'the rest of the world' – and thus also death as a complement to an individual's existence. My existence when I and my death become mutually engaged elements of a larger fate, a certain whole that has meaning and its annals where others also have their place: children, friends, trees.

We are incapable of looking in this way. That is why we are a culture of sympathetic 'neo-cannibals'.

On wonderment

Free falling is such a wondrous state during which no force has effect. It is a
state of complete freedom. Wonderment can in fact be compared to free falling.

Humans are not very good at coping with falling. Even free falling. Human
nature demands support – that is strength – one balancing the tendency to fall
demanded by gravitation. This state of equilibrium – the burden of weight
pulling us down and the hard ground underfoot allowing to avoid a fall – this is
the singular trait of our existential situation. We are not surprised when so, for it
is normality. A normality in which in fact we take no notice, consumed in a
purposeful and conscientious burrowing into a space (in truth along a two-
dimensional one) marked out by these forces.

When there is no ground underfoot we sense danger of such intensity that in
fact this overcomes the experience of wonderment. The testimony of those who
happened to survive an earthquake confirms that the shaking of the earth along
which one sets foot is one of the most terrifying human experiences.

Perhaps that is why man is afraid of being in wonder. A state in which the
mind falls into nothingness is rather too strongly associated with losing the
ground underfoot, by falling, which threatens death. But gravity does not affect
the mind! There were the human body inevitably plummets downwards, the
mind can stay motionless, in complete freedom... We, however, are afraid of
this. When we fall, in truth this fear is tied to the prospect of crashing once more
– hard against the ground. But when – in self wonder – we fall in thought, and
there is nothing waiting underfoot?

Wonderment is strictly tied to time. In our experience it appears suddenly,
like a friend who after all we know departed 18 years ago for the Antipodes, and
who suddenly emerges from around the corner on the street. Only a moment
before our mind – thanks to our eyes – took in one familiar after the other
image: the rundown fruit and vegetable market, the wall facing the street, an
advertising poster and suddenly, astonishment! Before our very eyes there
stands someone who has no right to be here. The unseen but permanent order
crumbles, one that defines the course of our thoughts. Borders burst, paths cave
in – for a moment unfinishedness emerges.

The lack of wonderment – ergo certainty – in a mysterious way is tied to
identity. The fact that our thoughts in their movement are a moment ahead of
objects that emerge, not fully made aware of intentions, ones that prepare a
resting place for objects in our internal world. A fact that confirms the coherence
of our existence and its unity with the order of the world. This, which astonishes
us, contradicts such a coherence and as a result, contradicts identity.

Naturally our mind has the ability to weave the wondrous with a spider web woven out of a familiar though true wonder as opposed to a delicate surprise, which leads so far that the thread of understanding breaks, does not suffice. That is why in being in wonder we in fact become distant from our selves, stand in the face of the emerging and unknown – and only this is present. We fade apart.

Babies whose identity is still rather weakly expressed, shamelessly find unceasing wonder. Thus their blissful chubby cheeks. It may be suspected that fear of being astonished is tied to an excessive attachment to one's identity. And often it is the case that in fact those who are rather insecure – strongly protesting otherwise – avoid wonderment like the proverbial... Everything for them is simple and obvious, while so called mystery is acknowledged with a disparaging twist of the mouth. At the attempt of surprising them with anything at all, they reply with a suppressed fear and externalised aggression. They have no appetite for surprise.

Wonderment leaves the one surprised open to one more danger. Thus at such a moment he takes unto himself his own image of the world, his identity – is suspended in his own state of weightlessness, devoid of the structure of judgements and belonging that protect. An easy prey. An astonished mind is a mind easily given a new dimension, caught in a web of ideas and explanations, be pinned to a concrete theory. That is why we eagerly express true wonderment. Naturally, there is no mention here of ironic surprise, being in essence an expression of sarcasm and distance. It is though an entirely different state. A person truly in wonder is like a child, for a short while defenceless. And it is risky to be defenceless in the presence of our kin. There is always the chance that someone shall wish to take us into their world, their structures and we, to defend ourselves, shall have to cast aside the blissful weightlessness of wonderment and don the armour of what we know, think and remember.

Even if we do not fear an invasion of others' thoughts, we avoid wonderment in the company of others, for it does not allow for communication. In order to communicate with others, one needs to return to language, to a discourse ordered in thoughts. This is a denial of wonderment. Only people bestowed with mutual great trust and at the same time able to communicate without words, can find wonder together. Just as so happens with those in the wonder of love.

That is why a mature person usually finds wonderment in their own company. They are then a poet, a mystic or scholar. Each of these engagements demands a moment in which a separation occurs from the familiar and a suspension into nothingness. A suspension of thought. Then all of a sudden it transpires that free falling does not threaten a catastrophe, for it is not a fall. And our ill-timed intuition that warned us about this, was but an illusion.

On smell

Smell in the kingdom of the senses takes up a singular position. It is therefore the most archaic and the signals it brings penetrate us through and through. The nerve apparatus construction itself that carries olfactory stimuli appears fossilised – something too simple, not corresponding in its construction to the refined structures of senses such as hearing or the kingly – on account of its dominating position – sight.

The olfactory bulbi are separated from the external world only by a delicate sieve of bones, which in this place turns out to be unusually thin. Further on the stimuli travel almost directly to the rhinencephalon. Of particular interest is the word itself 'rhinencephalon'. The description brings to mind something primal, blindly making its way forward, driven only by the most primitive instincts. And in fact, the rhinencephalon is the oldest part of the cortex, directly associated with centres of emotions that impose irrational and violent behaviour.

The relationship of olfactory stimuli and emotions reaches further. Emotion is a phenomenon of consciousness that never appears as a self sufficient entity, separated from all other feelings and therefore easily and clearly grasped. Emotions colour their – let's assume dark – tones in all phenomena grasped by the mind, giving them a unique hue. They create a space in which the theatre of thought and perception plays out. So as to thought as such, it must become named in words and changed into a lifeless, desiccated shell.

So too in the case of smell. In contrast to the other senses, it does not present ready-made elements. When sight reveals objects, and hearing sounds or melodies, smell rather engulfs us in an undefined sensation, emitting an unclear signal that is followed by something more concrete. Smell does not make itself distinct from a background – it is the smell that creates background. This consequently means that it in fact achieves a deeper so called penetration than images or defined sounds. These allow for taking a main position that places the object seen somewhere opposite, at a certain distance. Smell permeates into us, penetrates the defences that we establish so they secure us in the face of the foreign – penetrates the boundary of the I. This strength of penetration and archaic regions that it activates in us in a particular way define the position of smell among the senses.

Receiving signals from others, we define our position in relation to them. When I look at someone, I allow for them to influence me by their appearance. Their dress, charm, expression of eyes or how the mouth is set – all shape an image that can engage sympathy of deliver dislike. That something carried by sight, appearance, plays an enormous role in shaping mutual chemistry, though – to a certain extent – it is not considered as intimate. We have lived to see the day when even the most extravagant outfit such as metal in the ear and nose, enormous tattoos on the shoulders, light green hair and wedge-heel runners and even a – two-piece suit, are not considered strange or at all reprehensible. Rather, they serve as a beacon that says I am this and that, embody this and that style.

It is possible therefore to be a punk, NWCJ (New Wave Catholic Journalist), skinhead or hobo. None of your business, I can be anyone I want to be... There is a huge freedom to shape one's image – one that is carried by sight. This has, after all, an important function in organising the social fabric. The distance therefore that the visual relation ensures, guarantees one is untouchable. Across the world in which we are surrounded by unending human versions of appearance – on screens, billboards and posters – in fact the image loses traits of personal function, ceases to be the relation of man with man, becomes a calling card on exhibit to all and sundry. Perhaps though a deep devaluation of appearance is tied to this?

On the opposite end is touch. In our civilisation touching is strictly forbidden. In as much as it terrifies us, the most eccentric aesthetics of others is in principle allowed, though trespassing the magic circle of 20 centimetres that everyone draws around themselves, demands a formal permission. And if, however, by accident – profuse apologies. Bumping into one another in the bus, touching someone's hand in the shop or panting into someone's collar are situations that embarrass.

It can be suspected that these models are related to violent emotions such as touch can evoke, most of all the impulse of aggression and desire. Touch causes a strong reaction. It is atavistic. It does not organise a complicated social behaviour such as appearance but a sudden, forceful reaction of one being against another. For if someone is touched, they are also defenceless. It is easy to inflict pain or subjugate them.

The specific nature of smell lies somewhere in between two extreme senses. The fact that it functions across a certain distance distinguishes it from touch but links it to sight and hearing. Its atavistic nature though, the fact that it drives deeply and instinctively, makes it similar to touch. The homeless who stink, are treated as someone who takes the liberty to touch us with their dirt and poverty. If only they looked unkempt! But they stink. This cannot be tolerated. It could pass on, as in making contact.

Fortunately pleasant smells also have a far-reaching effect. A little mist of perfume is like a delicate, direct contact, a hint of a brush along the back of someone close. Intimate signals, personal, whose appearance no longer carry, flow today thanks to smells. Rhinencephalon, more strongly than we realize from day to day, has an effect on our basic mood.

From beyond the grave

Mr. P. thinks about the Polish Reprivatisation Bill. What is its connection and
the issue of vampirism? Well, he thinks, there is. He can demonstrate this.
Starting from those who in French are known as *les revenants* – the returnees.

The dead who return awaken a panic-stricken fear in the living. In
traditional folk sensibilities this type of supernatural beings are most vividly
'branded' and the most dangerous. The vampire, phantom or demon raise fear –
more than a match for water nymphs and water elves.

And why is that so in fact? After all, we are speaking of our beloved dead,
visit them on their day of remembrance, consult them in our thoughts on
difficult matters. In many religions the forebears are honoured almost as gods.
So what harm would it do to meet them? Therefore we respect them as long as
they are in the grave. At least, on the other side. On that side, not on this. This is
ours. And there is no place here now for them.

Ludwik Stomma, ethnologist writes, that the belief in the resurrection of the
dead is only possible based on a sign that they have not yet risen from the dead,
the time has not yet come and that for now they are still as dead as they can be.
Otherwise therefore the division of competencies would vanish, institutions
would cease to exist and there would be a destruction of the natural, holy order
of the world. It is not without reason therefore that the living after death are, in
the logic of mythical thought, now demons, phantoms, vampires – beings that
are harbingers – like all creatures that are mediums – of the threat of the world's
destruction.

Contemporary cinema eagerly makes use of this almost instinctive dread.
Scenes depicting dozens of corpses slowly crawling out of their graves, heading
in the direction of the town have now become part of horror canon. Not only
after all, in the modern age. Breugle's Apocalypses depict crowds of skeletons
falling on us, the few living.

Of importance is the leitmotif that returns in these dramatisations. The living
are few, defined and embedded in the normalness of the light, place, warmth.
The dead are many, an uncountable number of bodies spilling out of dark
crevices, holes, behind the lines of our world – bodies that take our places. And
it is not possible to kill them, for they have already died! And that is why as
writes Stomma, every now and then using the excuse of 'eternal memory',
'remembrance day of the dead' etc, we come to see if they had not escaped, to
check that nothing disturbed the sacred nature of things, whether we are the
rightful heirs.

There is the rub. We are the heirs. We are heirs to entire generations, several
ever less sensitive, vanishing into the dark figures. Now we have taken their

place! We live in their homes, we are husbands, fathers – and thus have taken also their place in the structure of existence. The return of the dead would threaten our place in the world. How many fathers would wish to all of a sudden take the place reserved for a father? How many dead people, deprived of their life (would they still be people?) would begin to take up our places at the table, in bed?

And in fact because those who already had their life – now stripped of the aim that saw their road to the very end, the dead can only be a threat. In essence, they can no longer take up our world; they have lived their own. They can only destroy it. Destroy through a jealousy of what they have lost, what has been lost for them. The world. Their world. That is we sense their evil, sense why they evoke such a panic-stricken dread.

And the matter of reprivatisation. A second expropriation. Taking the property of the living by those returning from beyond the grave, from the Shoah.

After all, they were removed from life with such laboured difficulty! Shot, gassed, thrown out of trains, stoned, eyes put out and stomach ripped open – with fearful monotony. Some though survived. Those that were already in the zone of death returned home, but others already lived there. And these others in no uncertain terms demonstrated that there is no place for you here. Do not return. Die – disappear...

At this point, thinks Mr P., one usually speaks of the war period as a reversal of civilisation towards barbarity. Or of appalling Polish anti-semitism. Or about the fact that these are just exceptions – in general people helped, taking the example of the clandestine Council for Aiding Jews, Żegota. Or that the poor took the Jew's wealth and would not return it.

Mr P. searches to understand. To understand how it's possible that starved and lonely, the blackened returned to their homes and evoked such fear and hatred. That others resorted to tying them to doors and putting their eyes out. He would like to understand – for it makes him anxious. And none of the above, the above that in fact does not explain anything, will change this.

So, it is easier therefore to understand that people who went about constructing a new life after a cataclysm, in fact looked upon these blackened figures as revenants, returning from the other world. They had already taken their place, taken their homes and bedding – that world had undergone total destruction, and here all of a sudden there appears someone from that world. A phantom. A blackened ghost whose presence in itself puts in doubt the new order. It is necessary to send it back to its world, return the scheme of things. It is necessary to kill them.

And a fearful anxiety remains.

The right to hatred

The second half of the 20th c. was a time of a great revindication of human rights. From the time when in the New York Declaration such rights were defined, other groups, nations and tribes – more, individuals, even states of spirit and parts of the body, began to demand the right for respect, love, recognition, the right to one's state or rightful place in representative organs. From the establishment of the western nation's wealth and explosion of decolonialisation movements in the 1950's, through to the *freedom fighters* of the 1960's, the carnival at the start of the 1970's, feminism, opposition movements and 'Solidarity' in the eastern bloc, multiculturalism and open demands for the rights of sexual minorities at the close of the 1990's and finally, the "Occupy..." movements, fruits of the economic crisis, connected with the Arab spring; liberty is marching on as if to the script of Tocqueville.

It has turned out that people have the right to organise and dress as they wish and make love or take up partners – without limitations of feelings, point of view. It would seem that now anything goes. But that is not the case. A certain part of human experience is encircled by a powerful sense of taboo – forbidden and condemned. One must not hate. One must not hold in contempt. One must not wallow in the humiliation of others.

And it is difficult to live without hatred.

In all cultures, throughout the ages, contempt for those who are lower placed was for many the basic source of satisfaction and joy. Moreover, the experience of positive and negative passions whose source was their place in the hierarchy, was and often still is the axis around which the entire social experience and order is based. As in the case of wolves who – when not hungry – love to play games of establishing position in the herd, chase the omega wolf and fawn on the alfa. So too humans fill their time lording over the weaker and toadying to the powerful.

There where people did not have anything, no form of joy apart from imagined hierarchies, the passions associated with these could replace all others and give human life a meaning. And though it would seem that the revindication of freedoms in the past half century or so is consistently breaking former hierarchies – stripping people of the pleasure and fear tied to humiliating others – not a lot is required for a movement back again. Germany, humiliated in its defeat in WWI and the poverty of the 1930's, was able to liberate itself within an enormous power feeding on the illusion of superiority and contempt of others. The psychological mechanism at the heart of Russia's power during Stalin's reign, was a similar phenomenon.

After its experience with totalitarian regimes a frightened democracy and tied to this a contemplative one, decided to strip people of the power to hate each other mutually. Appeals for it to root out this emotion, *please speak of everything but this,* meant that expressing this state of spirit became wrought with difficulty. One should always pray, as in the prayer young Mr. P. sung at the time of democratic opposition against communism: "...but do protect me, Lord, from hatred, /do watch over me that I do not fall into contempt, Lord..."

The democratic elites of the West made an attempt to remove parties and movements using the discourse of hatred from the media and wider public space – in addition, open calls for such were prohibited by legislation in many countries. In fact it ought to be said that these attempts are justified and no doubt even essential since hatred is appalling and a form of collective stupefaction. After the experience of a hundred bloodbaths, can one allow for a call for more? One cannot. Even if it were known forbidding such has no effect.

The conviction that a ban is justified is accompanied by the worrying awareness that it is not possible to ban something that has its place in the order of things. The crux of the matter is what this place is. The broadly accepted interpretation in the humanities discourse presumes a reactive, secondary nature of hatred. "When there is nothing else left, hatred allows one to proudly hold one's head high". These words by someone terribly hurt, remind that hatred has its purpose. Interestingly, a similar intuition can be found in the advice from poet and moralist Zbigniew Herbert: "... and do not forgive...". For those who feel humiliated and helpless, hatred is the most commonly accessible means of protecting an already disturbed sense of respect.

There is hope nonetheless that this means of justifying the stubborn presence of hatred is characterised by a certain naive faith in the fundamental rationality and innocence of man. Hatred according to this interpretation is a response to the hurt – maybe the easiest and most primitive of answers – though still an answer. If there were less hurt, if people were given more constructive means of demonstrating their rights, they would forget about hatred.

Or perhaps not? Perhaps hatred is not reactive? Perhaps it is self-sufficient, has its place in the spirit, a place where nothing can replace it? This is a worrying thought – though, as apologists of hatred maintain – is there anything greater than the sweet glory of victory against the enemy? Hatred allows to experience a moment of Nietzchean power, experience ecstasy, one difficult in the normal course of life. No doubt if one wishes to live without hatred, in harmony with the commandment of love, it is necessary to forego this appalling emotion of excitement. The state that ancient Germans attributed to warriors in the thrall of war's frenzy, known as *berkserk*. If that is the case, then there is no denying that the elimination of hatred in life is a true form of self-denial.

In fact hatred and contempt for those who are seen as worse can replace almost all sources of satisfaction. The experience of totalitarian societies informs that it is enough to give a person (at least many of us) the opportunity to torment their fellow human so that practically little else is necessary to be happy. This applies after all not only to totalitarian societies. Spartans hunting Helots for example. Young men from German *maennersbund* preying on strangers. Local councillors from Rhine villages selecting midwives and female herbalists as candidates for witches. A village group of larrikins breaking the nose of all and sundry who venture their way. The poor whites in Alabama holding blacks in contempt, even when they are being hanged. Middle management engaged in *mobbing* those in their charge.

It is possible to go on giving example after example. Mr. P. notes that in this regard Poles do not differ greatly from others. For many, one of the fundaments of national identity and human respect is the right to extol hatred towards the Russians, Germans and most of all, Jews. And suspicion towards all who refuse this right. For them in fact, political movements are divided into patriotic, meaning allowing to hate and those that have betrayed – those forbidding hatred.

Slowly but surely the terrifying memory of danger that unbridled hatred brings is being eroded. Ever more often political leaders speak to this emotion, ever more often their discourse turns out to be effective. Everyday life, t o o r e a l t o b e g r e a t, lends itself closer towards a dark abyss. As a result those longing for hatred ever more often caste aside moralising humanists who take away their right to ecstatic episodes of contempt.

Those, thinks Mr. P., who believe in democracy, who defend reason and peace have to continue doing their work – patiently warning of the ecstasy that brings death. They should not wonder, however, if they are punished for this through a defeat at the elections. They are demanding therefore a great sacrifice from others, a sacrifice from an integral part of their very selves.

On cruelty, a reprise

Cruelty creates a special sense of fear. A condition in which awareness denies what appears, negates it, rejects, and at the same time is totally helpless in the face of it. Cruelty paralyses – in fact because on the one hand awareness does not wish to accept it and on the other, it imposes itself and does not allow to be removed, forgotten. There is no better example of the Lacanian predominance of the signifier.

The presence of cruelty is a fact that proves unusually stubborn, one that constantly returns. From the Ancient World of nailing the living to the cross, up to contemporary times where the living are impaled. Man is savage. Thus where does the stubborn closing of the eyes come from, one that appears for example in calling someone cruel 'inhuman'?

The majority of us have experienced the taste of our own cruelty. Almost every boy has tortured insects or amphibians – flies, frogs. Some, also cats or dogs. Those who did not, looked on in fascination and with a heart racing in repulsion, later choking with emotion, would recount this to others. I do not know many that stood up against such a practice. Girls at times, but for the life of me, I do not why. They are no less cruel – though somewhat in a different way.

How does the suffering of a frog inflated by a straw differ from the suffering of a human? I do not know, do not know of a measure by which the pain of torn apart insides can be assessed. I know the pain that comes with trying to correct a twisted joint. A nightmare, where the whole world disappears, turns into pain, into waves of pain – and nothing can take its place, a great world of pain, an entire world with mountains and oceans of pain.

And the feeling that it must end at once, it must! There is no choice – but it does not end. The pain endures. A state of alienation where no one else knows, knows what is really happening. Nor does anyone else feel this. I am absolutely alone. Around me there are white hands and green aprons, faces concentrated and faces talking – but in another zone. They are not in my cosmos, do not exist for they are not a part of the pain, real pain.

He who suffers, suffers in the extreme, is isolated. His pain cannot become something in common, is not subject to mediation. Words, the basic instruments of creating a common world of people, do not bring physical pain. That is why a tormented person is like a tormented animal – howls, salivates and pleads with their eyes. The very fact of being a victim means being exiled from the world of people. Extreme cruelty does not differentiate victims in any positive sense. It leads to extreme bestiality.

The rest, the belief that the tormentor with every blow endows his victim with an identity and drags them beyond their very self whilst themselves diminishing, increasingly more powerless a villain who cannot attain their goal, as claims Jolanta Brach-Czaina, a philosopher, is an attempt at mediation, an attempt at reversing values. In the area of facts – not signifiers – the lout thrashing the passer by, taking their wallet does not diminish but grows. Just as the lion devouring a gazelle. And only our will to defy cruelty can reverse these values. Through the creation of myth. A myth that gives value to weakness, as does Christianity, or a myth that says the fact itself of man's existence has the right to respect its body and physical safety. The ethics and rights of man can be – though do not need to be at all – the emanation of our will to deny cruelty. But certainly are not something that is given to us, or revealed further by our intellect. Here the guide is Nietzsche.

Great crimes are not needed to know this. A sufficiently frightening testimony to the above is the world of children where they govern with their own laws. In this world the child that allows to be tormented and allows to become a howling victim, so other children see this, ceases to be a human. They will no longer forgive it – it shall become 'the one' that embodied suffering and not 'someone'. Everyone who knows what orphanages are, boarding houses or corrective school, knows this. The victim becomes a collaborator of the tormentor in the act of dehumanisation.

In a way similar to the way it paralyses awareness, cruelty goes against the grain of anthropology, all means of rational justification that the human family is a type of community. In the light of cruelty such attempts are pitiful. Only blindness demanding to renew these attempts with such self-importance becomes a source of surprise. This is tied to the above discussed tendency to deny, casting cruelty beyond the realm of discourse and its related thinking. Cruelty must be condemned, for the attempt to mediate it in sociological or anthropological discourse – an attempt to understand it – means coming to terms with the fundamental assumptions of our thinking about our selves. It is this fundamental assumption that it endangers.

The thesis of all anthropology is that there is a certain universal, particular property that is the essence of humanity and this property is not just a matter of being a biped but is also a guarantee of a certain community that is felt by one person to another. How is this thesis reconcilable with the fact that one puts out the other's eyes, glorifying in the howling of his fellow human?

And what does it mean that those of us who do not torture anyone without any particular emotion of the spirit, can every now and then watch scenes of butchery somewhere in Africa? Thus either we refuse to allow this cruelty to enter our thinking and experience and then for our awareness it means as much as coloured blobs on the television screen, or we also glory in suffering and violence.

Even if the first thesis is true, if we do not glory in cruelty but reject it, we create an ambiguous situation – for we are casting beyond the pale of humanity both the perpetrator and the victim. The fact that we can look at piles of Tutsi with heads axed means that to some degree we do not sense a community with these Tutsi. These are a species of far-away beings who met such a hostile fate. With their murderers the Hutu, we don't have anything in common either – these are bloodthirsty monsters, barbarians. Humanity, its universal value is protected and pure – cruelty in fact occurs beyond the family of mankind. It is the domain of inhuman monsters and their abstract victims.

Let us repeat. Thinking based on the assumption of the existence of a certain universal, objective human community that exists cannot come to terms with the image of a Serb of the last decade of 20th century, who upon leaving home kisses his mother's hand and then goes on to rape another woman, slitting open her stomach. Such a line of thought forces us to negate facts, to throw this Serb beyond the bounds of our community: Serbs are savage, only scum and only the mentally ill resort to such acts. It gives the human community the category of 'human', the status of something that exists objectively, something that is to protect us from non-human behaviour. Though it does not. Cruelty continues to return in defiance – and refutes anthropology.

In maintaining this stereotype popular culture plays a significant role. In the films like *Schindler's List*, mass murder strikes someone 'else'. Those who we come to know, those who we allow into our world, with whom we somehow identify, are saved. Only the anonymous perish. That is why Mr P. believes the film does not narrate the truth but sustains a soothing myth. If Spielberg had introduced a great many protagonists, allowed us to love each, to understand, empathise and then had shown that all, literally all with the exception of one had perished – and Schindler saved only the one – and if he had shown as was the case later that someone had been speaking to shadows all their life, then perhaps he would have succeeded to narrate a fragment of truth. But this would have undermined myth too strongly, a myth that spoke of death and cruelty, in truth affecting only others.

I therefore think that paradoxically the anthropological view that states the universality of what is human, casting cruelty into the sphere of the non-human, unusual, exceptional, abnormal, bypasses an all-threatening reality, the permanent presence of cruelty. How in all of us it lies in waiting.

It is necessary therefore to construe cruelty in another way, rejecting assumptions of humanity on the outside of which sits cruelty. It is necessary to depart from fundamental experience, experience of a solipsistic consciousness for which all others, other people, their experience of life, pain, suffering are only phenomena that flow by. They appear, exist for a while and vanish. And it is necessary to recognise that for my consciousness – mine, yours, all of us – there rests the burden of imbuing these phenomena with meaning, rational, though even the most simple such as 'man'. And this is a burden for there is no community of meanings as a given.

Cruelty becomes understandable if we recognise that the world of the tormentor is absolutely separate and the victim is only a phenomenon of this world. The intention of the tormentor endows this phenomenon such meaning, one that justifies torture. And it truly makes no difference who its victim is. In the world of the tormentor it is only a correlate, object of attack, of an act of hatred, act of punishment, an act that gives the world of the tormentor a sense of order – entailed in the words 'my community'. Otherwise it is not possible to comprehend that a person ripping open the stomach of a pregnant woman, can have a sense of a well fulfilled responsibility.

In refuting anthropology and what it stands for, cruelty humbly shows that we live in separate worlds and that others are what they are for us (whether we see them as brethren in humanity, or monsters hidden in the guise of humans), depends on the tricks of our consciousness. All forms of human communion – as well as all exclusion, casting beyond the community – are but tricks of a lonely consciousness.

3. The war of icons

Catwalk

The models glide along the catwalk, high, above the heads of mere mortals, faces lit by the lightening of cameras flashing, faces frozen in gravity. Smiling very rarely and as long as the ritual lasts, the smile falls towards the audience like a sign of grace. Not until the music dies and there appears a great priest, Versace or Kenzo – veritable gods – do the models now turned giggling girls, nestle up to him, waving at the craned necks of lenses zooming in. This though, no longer belongs to the very rub of ritual.

That is the picture. Fashion parade – a passion play in reverence of a secret deity. How else to explain the surprising force of the world of fashion? What would this heaven-bound elevation mean – a model, a woman in whom fashion is *revelation*? Why is her face anchored in infinity and why is she a picture of icy calm, a distance cold to all that is below, at her gliding feet – in a different world? Distance, to the publishers of 'Vanity Fair' or 'Vogue' bidding for her bodily charms, photographers-in-grotesque, veritable mascarons, contortionists capturing the beauty passing high above, and politicians calculating the gains that beauty can bring.

Thus the Greek gods unveiled themselves to man. Thus grey-eyed Athena unveiled herself when she stood behind Ajax.

A simple sleight of giving. Woman after woman, always young, emerges from the dark, steps towards the podium edge, there where the hungry bright lights of cameras wait. Walking the catwalk to appease the hunger of countless viewers, eyes glued to the screen. The climax, beauty ought to be thrown to the lions but a carefully studied move, a turn and now a return for a moment to keep her captors captive, in the end only to dissolve into the beckoning dark and return anew, for that very moment to appease the emptiness of glances.

She has an absent expression, unseeing, eyes aimed somewhere into the distance, a twist of arrogance. She looks down at the world an enigma, gravity free of emotion. Her eyes must not recognise anyone, glance uncertainly or mirror the faces dotting the audience – they must not even flit from object to object quickly, a move typical for studied observation. Who would she be therefore, should she glance at someone, focus her attention? She would then belong, to some one or some thing. Yet she doesn't belong to anyone; rather everyone belongs to her, voyeur-captives, taken whole, by her heavenly, pulsating walk. She is beauty. Her charm is not of this world but carved with earthly light, robes, flow on flow, face a palette of ochres. She does not belong, gives herself, her gaze though absent flows across everyone and everything, cutting through all and sundry. Beauty falls in cascades into the world, visible for all alike but not given to anyone.

The ritual of the gaze. Beauty, the promised land of happiness.

Hierophany, or fashion according to pre-modern times

In the secularized world awakening religious ecstasy in mystagogues and fear of God, hierarchy laid out in dimension, the play of light, rising coils of smoke and finally music, all harnessed for the theatre of dress and undress. Why? The first, simpler answer is that for the dictators of fashion what is good is what increases sales. To this end leads the stoking of bonfires to a quasi-religious state of emotions at promotional events such as the catwalk. Rapture, excitement – all is encoded in the memory of millions and the very next day will lead them to the nearest *prêt-a-porter* where they buy so as to take on the guise of deities.

Here though, another mystery lies concealed. Why therefore do fashion parades and similar events, such as award ceremonies for the most famous impersonators or the most beautiful women, in general arouse so much emotion, excitement or simply ecstasy? And, changing somewhat the order of the question, why is it these and not other events that have become universal rites of initiation for our present-day civilisation? Anyone though, who attempts to mock this world, manages only to ridicule certain people or certain situations. Although one may deride the empty veneer of glossy magazines and the vanity of dictators of fashion one will, however, be unable to put the mystery to rest. It is possible therefore to humiliate these high priests, to reveal the rituals backstage but in the practice of the cult there is something that always remains, which laughter and common sense cannot reach.

According to Rudolf Otto: 'It will be our endeavour to suggest this unnamed something to the reader as far as we may, so that he may himself feel it. There is no religion in which it does not live as the real innermost core, and without it no religion would be worthy of the name'.[5] Here the emotional nature of *numinosum* revealing itself is important. The presence of idols is for man a type of spiritual state – an emotion that is a sign. A sign that points to that sphere of existence that really is, but is unseen under the mask of *plethora*.

And what happens to this feeling when there are no idols? When – as for most of the West – God is dead? When none of the elements of being appear to possess that privileged position reserved for idols? Does this emotion also vanish?

No, it cannot. It is after all, a part of the human spirit's backbone. Just as Otto, who attempts to help the reader to rediscover it in their own self – just as Eliade who tracks it in the cultural vogues of our time, we rediscover its artistic presence in great mass-culture celebrations. And ask, why in fact there, on Paris and Milan catwalks does excitement and ecstasy again rear its head? Artistic

---

5   *The Idea of the Holy.* Trans. John W. Harvey. [*Das Heilige*, 1917] Oxford: Oxford University Press, 1923; 2nd ed., 1950:6.

revelation. The arts of the age most fully express the hidden understanding of being and its form, which this epoch construes. Hieratic statues of ancient temples in Egypt expressed the weight and gravity of the other worlds that crushed the living. It was not the *techne* of the artisans that defined the nature of those sculptures. This was an intentional message – surely an obvious and the only possible one for the temple slave – that determined technique.

Several centuries later, perspective was not the artisans' invention that came to revolutionise the vision of the world for Renaissance man. Rather, it was the change of that vision, loss of interest in painting depicting the transcendence that forced the discovery of perspective.

This reasoning on the part of Malraux, it should be said one that is essentially Platonic, leads us to the question: what type of ritual is conducted during a fashion parade? What intuition of form is concealed in this cult? What is the basic, fundamental, determinist act of existence for all those that belong to this cult? Just as death and life after death – as it appears to us – was the essence of life for Egyptians, so too something must unite all who with deadly earnestness sanctify the *prêt-a-porter*.

All the more that any expression of faith relating to the absolute has been made relative. Today every discourse – also that of religion – is conditioned by the hidden interests of those who espouse it, set historically, a symbol of its times. The absolute and universal has to be therefore beyond discourse. It is no coincidence that the 20th c. theological fundament of religiosity has been set in the sense of *numinous*. This allows reaching beyond the sourcerful thicket of ideas, mirrored reflections, masks and simulacra. The absolute is non-conceptual.

The non-conceptual is how beauty affects us. Kant expressed this in stating that the emotion beauty awakens in us is devoid of rules but all the same, necessary and widespread. And that is fact. It takes one's breath away and clouds reason. Smites. By means of this precision of emotion, necessity and universality without form, the emotion of aesthetics is related to the emotion of *numinosum*. And that is why in a world where every discourse can be made relative, the emotion of aesthetics remains the shelter of the absolute.

In this way therefore the most paradoxical form of identity has arisen. When the critical mind undermined belief in what is not manifest, it took on the mask of the golden calf so as to return to the human spirit. Thus whether we wish to or not, it has its place there. For we have exiled it out of our world, it has joined forces in an absurd, impossible alliance with its eternal rival – the golden calf, idol, Baal. Worshipped in fact because it is visible, glorious and beautiful. And because with appearance it is not necessary to guess at all, not necessary to confess as purportedly did Tertullian, *credo quia absurdum*.

Appearance of the Gazed has become the shelter of *numinosum*. The catwalk though, is the expression of appearance as the Ideal. This Ideal sets foot on earth. For a while Beauty personified in woman makes its presence among us. Above our heads, stops and returns, several more steps, then vanishes backstage. The model's journey along the catwalk becomes hierophany.

What can the acolyte do in order to take part in a cult? For millennia the answer has been the same – to identify the image in what is most essential for that idol. Repeat the holy narrative. The storylines differ though, for they relate to various structures of being. Australian aborigines roam in the spaces marked out by the deeds of mythical forebears, repeating their heroic deeds that once created the land. A disciple of Hinduism, through living life according to ritual, takes part in maintaining the existing order whose guarantee is the daily sacrifice offered by the Brahman.

And therefore the sun rises, rain falls. Through the participation of sacrifice the Hindu forms a dam against chaos. The Christian takes part in the act of salvation. In the image of the saints, throughout and through his life increases the store of good – and thus forms a dam against Satan. In the period set on the one hand by Creation and Sacrifice, and on the other by the Final Judgment, he takes part in the struggle of good against evil.

In the cult of the Gazed that personifies Beauty, the faithful grapple with old age, disintegration, ugliness. As well as forgetting, which falls into a state of loneliness? Grapples with the inevitability of time passing, one that erases all presence. Through a striving for godliness it has the opportunity to belong to something that transgresses its individual fate. And to be in a much more intensive means than when it is not alike anyone.

For Beauty lives in eternity and the passing of time is its counterpoint. Being one with the ideal, the faithful manages through the purchase of their own Gazed attributes. By purchasing one can be alike a godly image. Taking part in the Gazed that reaches for a detached self. One that for a moment permits to stop the passing of time – to be in eternity. It is these few moments when the model sails over the heads of the faithful. Any moment now she will vanish backstage – and then fall into non-memory.

Time, or fashion according to modernity

In a world governed by clocks, fashion in its own way gives testimony to the passing of time. It is in fact this that it serves, thanks to which the hand running from the past to the future is before our very eyes. One that almost at the same time permeates and is made manifest by minds in the fashionable figures on billboards and the covers of lifestyle magazines, the less modern, passed in the crowd on the street, sitting in the metro or in cars and the completely not modern to be found on right-bank railway stations buying three apples at the housing estate stall or taking the iron to be fixed. All of these flow into one, showing time in the from-to of passing, direction, where to look for the new and where the old piles up in lifeless puddles.

As the historian of ideas, Norbert Elias claims, chronometers serve to join into one equally flowing – devoid of individual traits – means of absolutely non reducible existence and time of particular beings. Thanks to the ticking of clocks, merchants sailing the seas lived in the same reality as did foremen of factory workshops while money lenders sitting by their abacus could arrange the baker's credit for eleven o'clock – who by three in the afternoon paid for the flour so that before dawn bread could be baked for the workers, for whom in turn the factory siren was a necessary and at the same time, a good enough clock. All this in the relatively still little complicated 19th c.

The time of clocks though is in fact by definition devoid of any traits of quality. Only an ascribed number differentiates a moment from another moment, shown on the face by equally moving hands or dashes changing configuration on a LCD miniature screen. Nothing on the face indicates in which direction time should flow, which moment is better than the other, there is nothing that would allow a universality of common time to be dressed in particular but also at the same time, universally recognisable traits so as some moment in the past decade be for all one of purple, one of trousers and hat, one of those dances and stars' lips meeting at that time.

Modernity in joining completely various worlds of particular people, their completely personal experience of days and years passing into one, common for all dimension of time, had to strip this dimension of all particular traits understood for one group of people, and hermetic for others. Time was to be the same for all – its bombardment of signs tied to religion or tradition of this or other culture was increasingly pushed aside to the margin. For a banker lending for a percentage the cyclical time of the world and religious fasts had – and has – a separate meaning, in fact not reducible to the only important timing, an equal time of capital growing, growing power and possibilities whose number is ever increasing. Regardless what emotions and experiences accompany the decoration of Christmas trees. Or slaughtering the lamb on Ramadan, funerals of close ones, weddings and births, morning news about wars or theatre reviews. In this equally measured approximation, growth, unchecked and uniform self completion known as progress, beats the strongest heartbeat of modernity – its true religion and faith, its existence. Ascetic and focused on one goal. All others are a matter of folklore, something needed to entertain children.

The clock is a splendid manifestation of the ascetic faith of modernity. But the clock will not suffice. It will not suffice to continually peer at the numbers that total, marking more seconds, minutes and hours. Signs are needed that tell of all of life's meanings but in a way that inscribes this story into the context of a modern faith, belief in the progress and superiority of the new over the old. And that is why in fact a modern way to apprehend fashion had to arise, a fashion that records all of life's riches in the one-way, linear passing of time. A fashion thanks to which at every moment, without a clock and calendar, walking along the street and perusing a newspaper, we see this passing.

We see it in the difference between yesterday's and today's line of motor cars, which we stop and look at. We see this in the surprising compositions of designers, yesterday adorned on catwalks by models, now though by students at seminars. After all there is now something new on catwalks, so by tomorrow, today's outfits will be a sign of a backwater, the archaic that fades into the distance of an ethnographic museum – while today's students already as if harried women, give way to new tides of students with a new cut here, an addition somewhere there.

We sense that passing in our own surprise when others use words in vogue only a few years back but ones we would no longer. Or when the merits of a book are debated, one whose author we no longer remember – for 'is there anyone who still talks about this...?', we sense in the rather cloying and at the same time lazy resonance of the verdict: 'it is *passé, passé* – let's move on to another topic' in the words of friends, or offered at supper: 'haven't you seen this yet – where have you been?' It is only thanks to this intimate tie with time, with a homogenous medium in which everything can be encountered – and has to be – with everything, that fashion can fulfil, which Georg Simmel outlined as a function that stratifies a seemingly united society.

Fashion, the passing towards the new, is everywhere and though it is the source of much silent suffering, anxiety of falling out of step and embarrassment when it occurs, it at the same time adds to substance through content, imbues with meaning; making a rite of the only serious expression of man's faith in the modern world.

Concentrating all our real attention on the one goal, on the growing passing of time known as progress, the modern world has risked a great deal. The passing hands that go around thus only show time's passing – while the growth, accumulation, inevitable approximation to the goal, in a word progress, this is all an expression of faith. A delicate and demanding confirmation. Fashion has fulfilled and perhaps will still play the role of such testimony, one confirming in the day-to-day, the superiority of the new.

But the fundament of this faith has already been washed away. Postmodernism, questioning the fact that the hands in turning push time forward in some defined direction, has deprived the ritual of fashion of a deep and metaphysical meaning. Paradoxically, it has not at all weakened it. After all, this paradox is only a seeming one, for it is known that a ritual in fact blossoms when it discards its metaphysical corset. A Baroque religiosity of rituals was possible when Blaise Pascal sensed the distancing of God. Thus the ritual of fashions and their theatre is growing – all chasing the new, for at the end of the day, it is sufficient to stubbornly repeat the gesture of faith, so that faith returns.

The war of the iconoclasts and iconodules

In the eighth century BC the Byzantine empire was torn apart by conflict leading to widespread bloodshed. A matter of icons. Iconoclasts, destroyers of images, determined that the spreading cult of holy images throughout the land was in fact a form of idolatry condemned by the Holy Bible. They claimed the Old Testament prohibited the reproduction of what was created as a likeness of the Creator and in the name of this prohibition, would kill all iconodules – those who painted the face of Christ and the saints. In temples they smashed mosaics and tore plaster off the walls, where it was possible to see the cloud-like presence of dignitaries 'transformed' by grace. This way they showed their faith in a God who is not manifest.

The iconodule believed that an icon itself contained an element of God – that contemplation of a holy image allows to look a God in the face. The iconoclast, however, was convinced that this is a foul heresy and that an earthly image distracts from the voice of God, which ought to be heard, though its source is at a distance of infinity. The attempt therefore to gaze into the eyes of God was considered as sheer arrogance, hubris for which one pays with the poverty of illusion that is directness. For behind the painted piece of board any moment now, there will be nothing but an appalling emptiness.

Today those who despise the modern culture of the West claim that it worships the golden calf. That it has forgotten God, forgotten all that is spiritual, forgotten that the groundwork of ethics has to be rooted in matters that are not witnessed. They claim the only desire of those in the West is one that rests in material gains. The West wishes to admire them, directly worship their accessible forms, wallow in their sensual presence, wade in their symbolic substitute – money. Martin Heidegger, a western thinker who despised the West, described the modern world as 'a time of the world of pictures'. Everything is an image, representation. What cannot be depicted, does not exist. Where the fundamental effort of people serves the visual, a world that is manifest.

An entire history of technology serves this purpose. Let us examine the telephone for example. Does it have anything to do with the dispute that ripped asunder Byzantium some 13 centuries ago? Naturally, contrary to appearances, it has. The telephone makes the present. Someone who is far away, someone not present, suddenly through their voice becomes so – within reach, right by our side. In the past – before the telephone was invented – in order to see the hazy outline of that person it was necessary to make an effort, remind ourselves or dream.

The screen makes the present even more so – making possible before our very eyes all that is distant or unseen. The world fills with images, voices, forms that fill human minds to the brim. There the koala spreads his elbows, a snippet from Australia by cable television or an image of a spleen, transmitted by an ultra-sonograph from the dark depths of the body. Not leaving any room practically for anything. Not even a small crack for longing.

The war with the West therefore is a war waged with the manifest world.

***

Let us return to the past. The iconoclast crisis broke out at a moment when Byzantium was struggling with dramatic difficulties. Exhausted by war through the centuries with Persia, with great difficulty it came to grips with the sudden expansion of Islam that posed a threat to the very existence of a Christian state. Continental Greece and the Balkan provinces were settled by pagan Slavs and Bulgars who were approaching the walls of Constantinople from the north. The remaining Byzantium loci of power in Italy, left to their own devices, led an independent existence, loosening ties with the centre.

The war with the Arabs was won by Emperor Leon III the Isaurian, and his soldiers from the east, close to the source of the Euphrates and Tigris, province of the empire. Some historians researching the conflict maintain the genealogy of these as having played an important part. This would explain the particular passion of the emperor and his hatred towards icons, as well as for the brethren worshipping them. The iconoclasm of this period arose therefore in fact in eastern Syria, somewhere on the borderlands of empires that had functioned for centuries.

The beginnings, it should be said, are shrouded in the distant past. As Leonid Ouspensky claims, theologian and icon researcher, Muslims in the first phase of their expansion were rather tolerant towards Christian images. At the same time though on the lands conquered by Islam, Jews began life anew and uncompromisingly observe the ban on worshipping images. Why? Maybe in the eyes of the new rulers they wished to distinguish themselves from Christians? This would seem though an explanation we should not place trust in. For in its political animus it is too dependent on our modern-world means of thinking. Perhaps in truth the issue was the ban? That appalling prohibition as a result of which Moses broke the first tablets when he saw the worshipper of the golden calf. Why would that prohibition reappear with such a strength? We do not know. It had to nonetheless, influence Christian communities and the disciples of the prophet himself. Not long after, the iconoclasts were already an influential group in the Omajjad state as in the Byzantium Empire.

***

The conflict over images is one those themes in culture that never disappear. Only to return, then hide under the cover of time and again appear several centuries later – in another region of the world, in another guise. It expresses a situation that cannot be resolved, a situation where there is always a line of thinking that attempts to impose a sense of order, looking for a vade mecum of instructions. The entire dilemma is related to the fleetingness of phenomena. Are we then destined to a dysfunctional pluralism of matters? To the fact of constant change, fleeting opportunities to grasp matters that flow in a stream that falls away into nothingness? Do we need to admit to the temporariness and inconsequence of all that comes to make up our world – and in the end our very selves? Or is there a chance we can anchor our contemplations in some permanent though not immediately palpable matter, which in fact lies at the basis of flux and therefore constitutes its principles?

If we therefore confess our faith into this absolute principle, unseen behind the plurality of phenomena, then how are we to make sense of it when all that can be made sense of, is always only another phenomenon? Does there not exist the risk that beholding the phenomenon, we forget about the principle that appears, which is represented? Perhaps therefore, putting faith into the hidden, transcendental, we have to resign from every means of relationship with this transcendentalism? What then is to be done with all the riches of the world that embark through the senses, beckon us through hearing, taste, touch and most of all – sight – eye of the spirit through which beauty calls? How to avoid the Pascalian distancing of God so it should not by chance amount to His absence? So that the loci of meta-reality to which we continually and repeatedly have to return in ungratifying labour not be replaced by emptiness. An emptiness in which the only hope and sense of relief are forms and colours in all their luxury and ravishing lack of shame.

***

Already in the fourth century some holy elders began to notice that the cult of icons is leading to excess. At times priests would conduct mass on icons, not on the altar. Zealous monks would scrape the paint from icons and add as a sacrifice to communion. Asterus of Amasia claimed that the embroidered imaginings of the saints ornament the holy dress of Byzantine aristocracy. In Alexandria ladies of society placed the representations of the saints on various parts of their dress! As if the culture of the Ancient World was still alive, a culture of image, one that had taken over Christian faith. Not able to overturn this through prohibition, seemingly accepting Christian faith, it deformed the new religion with a devotion to all that glittered, fancifully luxurious and blatantly visible. The reaction of iconoclasts was inevitable.

The eastern provinces of the Empire, borderlands where Greece and Syrians rubbed shoulders with Persians – was a land of Manichean heresy. It is there that iconoclasts could find a philosophical wellspring. Under the influence of Iran, theories were advanced that things and their shapes were the creation of an evil demiurge, as powerful as the good Lord or perhaps even more so – possessing such a force that entraps the spirit in a material body. Perhaps therefore from this point of view, in essence a Gnostic one, any attempt to presenting the image of God had always to finish as an act of idolatry. The image, the idol, presented after all the form and therefore the work, of a great demon.

Perhaps the soldiers of Leon III imbued with hatred towards the visual world, saw an evil there that arose in the corpus of the Christ church? And in the strength of the Muslims that had a great impact on them and towards which they had respect, they found in fact an uncompromising rejection of the earthly image, a strictly governed prohibition that allows the human mind not tie itself to anything. Only to God.

Let us look at this from another view. The cult of religious images was integrally tied to the monastic movement. Monasteries arose and multiplied like mushrooms in the Byzantine state and increasingly larger groups sought shelter there, thus searching in this way for the road to salvation. They sought shelter from the brutal pressure of taxes, from conscription, from a life laden with difficulties, closed in the circle of birth and death. It is in this way that we attempt to understand their choices.

Perhaps this concerns something less tangible? The emptiness of a secular life, lack of hope, meaningless existence crushed by a memory of a civilisation that is too old, boredom of theatre and games, pointless nature of philosophers' discussion who split the proverbial hair but in fact crave for distinctions and wealth? Perhaps of importance here is the loss of a sense of common fate that characterised the latter period of the Ancient World?

The cult of icons arose from the adoration given in large gatherings in Egypt and Palestine from time immemorial to the funerary portraits of great abbots and anchorites. It was around them that new communities arose. Was life that focused on the painting of a religious image without any importance apart from an attempt to portray holiness in colour and form, a better choice of road? Or for those who were not bestowed the art of 'writing' icons, contemplation itself, complete devotion of the mind, which can be seen through the play of colour and line, complete forgetting of oneself, one's bodily needs and human ambitions – could this not all represent a temptation to free oneself from the absence of hope?

To forget oneself so as to forget sadness?

***

In modern times it is claimed that the impetus for persecuting worshippers of images came from anxious bureaucrats of the empire army alarmed by the drainage of human resources to monasteries. Greek monks – in contrast to those of the West – did not farm the land, did not produce anything, did not build houses or walls. Worse still, they could not fight and Byzantium needed armies like a person needs oxygen. Finally, they did not reproduce – either peasants or future defenders of the state. They turned their backs on a dying state so as to contemplate the tar-black pupils of the Saints. This could explain the anger of the army, those who in the end fought and perished in battle.

Is the explanation again, however, not somewhat too contemporary? Does it not demand completion with that thin layer of thoughts and feelings, not entirely comprehensible to us – ones tied to the answer to the question: *W h e r e   i s   G o d ?* Where is true existence, one that is worthy of death and self sacrifice? And what is that sacrifice to be? Readiness for war sacrifice, shedding one's own blood – or also the ascetic in a break from the world in the name of contemplation?

Do warriors whose forays beyond their personal limitations, isolation – in a state where man becomes one with death – could they believe that the fervent prayers of monks had an equal importance? Were they not furious, seeing men in their prime cunningly beating their brows before a painted board? Not to mention the exaltation of women turning into bouts of fainting, as well as peasants crying before these idols – forgetting about the day-to-day where tears should be shed rather at the thought of the glowing embers of towns, torched by the enemy?

The fury must have been considerable. Practically no icons before the 8th c. – a time of icon destruction – have survived to this day. Bishops and the faithful who did not wish to join in to the acts of 'cleansing', were sentenced to torture and death. The Council from 754 called by the son of Leon III, Constantine V Kopronymos, decided that everyone who paints and keeps an icon at home shall be burdened with a curse. Those who resisted had their heads crushed, which were placed on the boards of paintings, others drowned in sewn up bags and the iconodules hands burnt so that they could no longer paint. Persecution continued in various degrees until the middle of the 9th c. when in 842 and 843, during the reign of Empress Theodora, a subsequent Council reinstated the cult of images, holding that on this occasion on the first Sunday of the Great Fast holiday of Orthodox Triumph, icons are to be worshipped.

***

The Feast of Orthodoxy. For Leonid Ouspensky, orthodox theologian, there could be no other orthodoxy beyond the one that reminds that for Christians, God embodied in his Son allowed himself to become known in the form of sight and touch. The icon therefore remains the most perfect embodiment of this fact.

In the icon the transcendental becomes manifest for us, in the will of God and according to holy history. The image remains a bridge to the other world and to us is neither entirely earthly, nor entirely foreign.

And if during that period in the 8th c. the will of iconoclasts had triumphed? Would Christianity have gone the way of Judaism and Islam? These two religions, turned towards the word and inscription, completely rejected the image. They state that between the order of the spirit and the bodily manifest there is a barrier that cannot be breached and that barrier must be kept – otherwise *sacrum* shall be subsumed and taken over by considerations of the material.

It is remarkable that this type of belief is tied to the spirituality of desert peoples. As if man only when standing in a boundlessness seared by the sun could go beyond what is visible. As if the one whose gaze does not rest on anything beyond the continually repeating patterns sculptured in sand by the wind, could begin to experience the intangible. The patriarchs gazing out into the burning sky and hearing the voice of the Lord. The Persians, wandering through their desiccated tablelands to realise the unseen tribulations of Ormuzd and Ahriman. Bedouins striking their foreheads towards the trembling posts of burning air. Only there, where there is nothing to distract the visual, can man see angels.

Byzantine iconoclasm showed another possibility. Emperor Constantine V Kopronymos, iconoclast, after destroying the cycle of evangelical representations in a Blachernae Church, ordered they be replaced with flowers and trees, featuring cranes, peacocks and crows. In the place of religious images there began to surreptitiously appear secular works of art, as if the sleeping spirit of the Ancient World had awoken.

That is how the fate of iconoclasm can be judged – appearing together with Protestantism in the western world. The God of Luther, mostly the God of Calvin, was so distant that through its incomprehensibility, arbitrariness, *t e r r i b l e   o t h e r n e s s*, it began to lose importance. In its place entered material things, the palpable, researched by science, modelled by art and foremost, produced thanks to human dexterity. One prepared from the times of the Gothic, exploding together with the Renaissance and its rapacious means of seeing the world, in the Enlightenment confined to the discipline of modern science, in the 19th c. enriched by the power of technology. Paradoxically it is that revolution that has led to the hypermarket becoming a temple and the catwalk, a ritual of sacrifice.

It is possible nonetheless to accept that the conflict between iconoclasts and iconodules is not a trap without any hope. That such an extreme iconoclasm as the modern culture of forms and appearance are poles towards which our thinking has wandered, remembering in itself in this forgetting and leading to extremes in its discursive thrusts, in the heat of the moment losing sense of proportion and balance. The sense of balance therefore lies deep in intuition, one like the problem of image itself, it returns through the ages in various forms. For the civilisation of eastern Christianity this sense was captured by the words of the Saint John of Damascus. After many centuries his thinking was enclosed in the Orthodox faith, accepted during the 7th Council, one that put to an end the period of iconoclasm. The elders teach: 'things that point to one another, undoubtedly also mark one another.' What appears to us is not entirely of the earth, but is not absolutely alien either. It is given so we turn our thoughts towards boundlessness.

Is it possible in the contemporary world to see things in their material form in such a way? Phenomena that take up our minds? Is it possible to see in them a pathway leading towards the transcendental, whichever way we wish to construe this, beyond the manifest world?

Palmers – voluptuous ads

Spring, so Mr. P.'s eyes stop more often at underwear advertisements. And so that it is worth stopping, the manufacturers make certain. Palmers, Triumph or Italian Fashion flood the townscape with images of young women in immodest poses, if not ones of shameless invitation. Will all the young men – thinks to himself Mr. P. – speeding through the town in their macho machines, manage to return home safely? More than one fixing his gaze on the tempting hips thrust at him, or following the line of thighs traversed by lace suspenders, will not notice the oncoming car – that in principle should not be there. A ready-made tragedy.

Opponents of immodesty attempt to fight underwear advertisements in various, usually ineffective ways. So they paint curvaceous backsides black. Glue over with old newspapers. Several weeks later billboards begin to blossom with another series of photographs. New feline females bend and flex their wares while their eyes of cold sensual disdain lock those in whom they awaken delight and those that awaken hatred.

The lack of impact in the war on billboards has many reasons. The first – and no doubt the most important – is the disproportion of funds. Clothing giants have huge resources and therefore hire advertising agencies, which in turn are not particularly bothered by the black blobs on previous versions of their work. Every few weeks or so another series is released that goes on to cover the 'improved upon' posters from before. From their point of view, the work of latter-day holy vandals destroying images is in fact desirable, like a moth to the light they bring potential consumers to this very product. In part, particularly among men, this 'vandalism' gives rise to a humble predilection to defend a beauty tarnished. This reaction is tied to the commonplace confusion in our culture – at least since the Renaissance – of Beauty and Good. Thus the undeniable charm of women dressed and undressed that manufacturers wish to sell, is as if bedraggled by the heartless swipe of a brush or the nondescript greyness of old newspapers that defenders of moral order, diligently glue over. The attack on Beauty is easily identified with the attack on Good, as well as an attack on the freedom of admiring the beautiful. An attack of ugliness, grey, provincial ugliness whose symbol becomes in fact a crumpled, yellowed newspaper.

It is easy in this place to forget that Beauty and Good are not one and the same. As Sören Kierkegaard wrote 'either-or... '.

Beauty of the body is inevitably tied to sex. With the call of sexuality that in a powerful way dominates other calls that people are prone to hear. Desmond Morris, an insightful observer of animals, writes of the dangerous power of sexual signals, signals that can initiate in humans forces that tear apart all social ties. From the point of view of the Montagues and Capulets fighting over the domination of Verona, the love of Romeo and Julia was destructive. It destroyed the order that was responsible for the social nature of the town, two houses, balance of influences and rivalry of social groups....

Can the motivations though that were responsible for the holy wrath of those who destroyed images be attributed to the protection of social ties endangered by matters of sexuality? This type of functional interpretation, no doubt true, nonetheless reveals something else. As in a psychological explanation, no doubt also true. One that explains this rage of frustrated desire, suppressed aggression of males or jealousy of some female in respect to others. All no doubt true. Though incomplete.

Does this though have a legitimate standing in respect to these eternal battles over covering and painting out advertisements of the flesh?

For Mr. P. that is not at all clear. The fact that the battle of those who create sublime images of the human body with those that cover it up has a deeper context, is testified to by the importance and scale of funds used for this purpose. There are serious doubts whether this part of the advertising dimension taken up by bras and stockings is proportionate to the market segment that in reality belongs to them. Does the average consumer devote to *lingerie* such a proportion of their attention and money or their partner's – as do advertisements – on women's panties, among all the street billboards?

This in fact traces a question mark. Mr. P. is rather convinced that advertising agencies wish to manifest the beauty of the body. More, he thinks that there are a great deal many people who wish to gaze at a living, arousing beauty. That in fact the art of advertising is but a pretext for a singular espousal of faith, for revealing the unseen: look, it is available, it is here, on earth, in form and shape... And in fact it is with this espousal of faith that iconoclasts wage battle.

And will they succeed? Rather not. Can they return the art of listening to the transcendental? Unlikely. They would need therefore to find a voice from the beyond that would drag us with great force, turn our eyes aside from form and shape that is Beauty. Alas, all they are able to do is cover over a Beauty in sin – with a yellowed newspaper.

Beauty on the other hand – regardless – remains the promise of happiness. Even if Beauty is a somewhat naked promise.

The mall

The huge shopping mall is like a small town. It has its streets, lanes, passages, arcades and places with benches. It has small cafes, restaurants, fountains, as-if street lamps, stairs (usually escalators) joining various levels, malls, *cul-de-sacs*... It has plants in pots, various trees, bushes and flowers, often creepers, at times plastic. And most of all shops, hundreds of shops and little shops all of a kind, each different, more charming than the other. The shops welcome, chat with the customer, look after him. At times the streets have names – Green, Violet, Pistachio written on the signs just as the names of these colours. On street intersections in the meantime, more or less amateur groups sing *country*.

Mr. P. is witnessing, how shopping malls mushroom in grey, often peripheral parts of large Polish cities, attempting to substitute their gaudy riches for the now absent shopping tradition and life centred around markets and arcade stalls. In substituting they do not reveal anything. Instead they generate a world that is in essence an illusion. Despite the fact that as a rule they are incomparably more beautiful than the old, shabby arcades. The point is that the shopping mall is, as Jean Baudrillard said, a *simulacrum*.

In the shopping mall, especially one recently built, everything is smooth and shining. Floors out of artificial stone, polished so as machines could easily wash and remove signs of mud brought in by thousands of passersby. Walls, separating particular spaces from one another, coated in paint, thanks to which some mysterious proportion of cations and anions repel grains of dust, keeping their freshness even after the passing of twenty-eight thousand hours. Banisters out of stainless steel, small chairs upholstered in leather imitation in colours that soothe the nerves, glass transparent as a cornea. Light from a contemporary lamp of the same length wave as natural light.

The shopping mall is similar to a small town. In fact the point is not about similarity but that it is a placebo. Thought up in America. Their natural context is a typical New World town. In the centre dominates the imposing CBD – *downtown* – filled with skyscrapers, one rather dangerous. Circumbracing also a continuum of endless sectors of family homes. There is no typical space of a traditional small town – small streets to walk, little squares and cafes. That is why the shopping mall replaces such a space, creates its fiction, deriving structure and directions but giving them a totally different meaning. In the bowels of such an as-if town, shopping mall, instead of a catacomb there is parking for cars.

Simulacrum – it is important to note, does not pretend reality. It substitutes reality. It feeds on an erased memory of form and shapes into which it has entered. Its power though is constructed on forgetting, on the impression that if it disappears itself then nothing shall remain. It is danger in-waiting, for it forces us to lend it more gravity than it has. A road sign to longing for that un-aware, offers its own inferior paths. In the shopping mall all these lead to the cash register. This place suggests implicitly that our *raison d'etre* is to be a shopper. The act of shopping hidden in the background of every gesture and step, reveals the seeming nature of this as-if space, thought up by interior designers. Passers-by though, think that everything is in its optimal place.

Some Europeans live in historical towns. They do not move house often. Usually spending a large part of their life in the one place, walking the same footpath, sitting on the same bench from time to time, in the company of unknown neighbours' gazes over long years. Naturally, the suburb is sometimes changed, even town or country, but the substance of these places continues. An old person sits on the bench by the market, under a huge tree whose crown was burnt by a thunder bolt. Forty years ago. He looks at those who only yesterday were children, greets their parents. Kindly looks out at tourists who are looking out at them, attempting to immortalise him on a photograph and the church in the background.

Tourists enter shops, buy tomatoes, smoked fish, or film for their camera. They buy from people whose features they would like to find in the face of figures presented in city museum frescoes. This somewhat gratuitous exaltation is justified by the state of the walls, wounds that time creates. This gives people a complexion, makes them worthy of spending time in centuries-old cellars where in the past, they ran their shops. The figures of saints adorning churches are eaten away by smog and in places where in the past there were eyes, now we find only shapeless hollows.

The shopping mall does not age. Before it manages to do so, bulldozers will pull it down and in its place, something else shall go up. Perhaps another shopping mall. Perhaps an office building. Or a sports centre. The short-term nature of the mall's existence borders on man-made eternity, characteristic for photography. This non-time aspect is reflected somehow in peoples' appearance, met in a shopping mall. Figures alike, they fill great advertising stills – smiling girls in jumpers, families celebrating their new jackets and scarves, serious men in suits or women in grey business outfits looking straight before them through glass, caught in elegant frames.

Usually a glance at other passersby – after all there are hundreds – is the only contact with others they are destined for. Fleeting images on the retina – here a man in a brown parker leans over a child, there a young couple – hair in various shades of fruit, further a lone figure, thin, in a grey coat. And still others and others who shall never be seen. They exist for each other alike signs, signifiers, alike the background whose most enduring part, part most repeated, are new designer brands.

That is why they don't differ so much from the figures out of advertising photos. Maybe even the latter are closer somehow. It is soothing in this veritable sea to again meet a familiar face, even if it smiles out of a photograph. Those out of advertising posters, mannequins, are in the shopping mall the most 'local' – it is they who populate this peculiar town. Remaining, when all others leave.

Mr. P. thinks, that the amazing success of shopping malls – constant, after all a companion of mass consumption society – in a place such as Warsaw, can in addition explain through its singular disability, the memory of its inhabitants. And perhaps even more through the disabled space of the city for whom memory is a scaffold. The power of *simulacrum* is related to the loss of the dimension of continuing, with the forgetting of reality stretched through time. One that as a sign, is to only follow. There where this memory is written in stone, where walls are old and people live among them from time immemorial, it is not so easy to deceive.

There however, where for some reason they forget about the past – or where they wish to forget it – it is otherwise. Where the past does not belong to anyone, where it is woven out of illusion, there *simulacrum* with ease barges in with its time-less, ostentatious arrogance. Against the background of grey high-rise flats shouting advertisements, against the background of the miniature old town and wedged here and there, burdensome skyscrapers, the smooth paths of the shopping mall can in fact appear true. All the more if they are to form a barrier from dark, sad and often fearful courtyards where our memory was raised. Perhaps it is time therefore to live in some or other *Shopping Centre*, on the corner, where we find the streets of Raspberry and Pistachio.

Metro

The metro joins every metropolis. The underground is universal, a civilisation constant that for all, as well as for various city spaces, provides an imprint in common – a signpost of 20th c. building giants. A city without a metro is irretrievably provincial. Travel by bus or tram is always a slow affair, forced by the lack of an underground world. When there is a metro, tourists take the bus, pensioners and those in love. Thus all those living life beyond the world that matters. Those who are not in a hurry. If therefore there is a metro in town this means people there are really all that is haste. And in fact haste manifests to us that life is essential, there is a lack of time for all the important matters out of which life is built.

A city where there is not a metro cannot pretend it is a capital, it undertakes important decisions, it hasn't time for the mountain of matters it has to deal with. No one shall believe. Like an unimportant clerk known to everyone, insignificant, though bearing the title of a senior official, even a small office with a desk. If the city was really important, if the mountain of matters demanded in fact a great haste, it would construct a metro for itself. Beyond doubt. That is why the residents of all capitals, asked which transport system they prefer, vote in droves for the metro. Contrary to widespread opinion, often completely rational, ecologists and urban planners claiming that an express tram or other solution would suffice. The gravity of a city that has a metro is made double.

Haste demands simplification. And the essential world is complicated. The world of a great metropolis is complicated beyond all possibility of human reasoning. The commonly known and impossible to solve problems in the organisation of a great city, from endowing it at least with such a right, somehow capturing its complex nature – hierarchy of beings, network of dependencies between all that exists in the world, points to this complexity as an integral trait of this organism. And the metro makes simple. A made simple reflection. Changes the pulsating riches of the city organism into a network of empty tunnels that join like-minded stations that differ only in the word. A city seen through the underground web of trains is a structure where loops differ only in the semantic. It brings all that is above ground to a unified space where we travel the metro, quanta, from the quantum state Père Lachaise to the quantum state Первомайская (Pervomayskaya). Through Wierzbno.

Metro stations have their own unique atmosphere. To be found always when taking the stairs down into the tunnel and at the same time, on the platform. The stations are underground, removed from the realm of clouds, rain and wind, trees, from history and architecture. They create the environment that is entirely artificial, more so than the tangle of streets on the surface. There man continues between sky and earth and even then when entering some gate after a moment daylight, at least through a windowpane. House and monuments are carved through history, atmosphere, through the character of the locals.

Not the metro. All the underground trains are similar, for – as mentioned – all are children of haste. And haste has no time for history, architecture or character. As it was said before, haste makes for the simple, the tried and trusted, procedure. Therefore all is artificial there – neon, plastic, steel or cement. And nothing can be done to change this. Typical as the fruitless efforts of urban planners with the aid of facade illustrations, glass cases or names to tie the nature of stations with that above ground, a fragment of city space. Figures of the revolution, painted on the walls of the Paris station Bastille or the Soviet Navy in bronze on some Moscow metro station look rather curious and out of place, melt with information tables and advertising fragments.

The underground therefore despite the intention to be a reflection of city space made simpler, cuts the umbilical cord. Distanced from above only by several, or a dozen or a few more metres, creates all the same its own world, where more familiar are similarities between the most distant station stops than between those stations and the street above, its firmament. In the world of trains underground everything is the world made simple, haste and imprint. Even people appear to be so.

They are at first glance. Though one must not be deceived. People in the metro are real. Beyond the made simple and frame – the real world of the metro is the crowd. Easy to miss this. In the end faces on the advertisements are more human than those that pass by on the escalators. Those passed though are real human faces.

It is no accident that the lonely like stations. On stations – a fact recorded many times – one is always among others. Loneliness at the station has yet another flavour. There everyone is away from home, anonymous, mutually foreign. So one more other, slowly making their way along the platform, peering into kiosks, eating a hamburger bought at the station take-away – is like any other. Is not any different. The metro though gives them something extra. In the metro they can confide in a train compartment, find a place and call it their own. They can rush on this place somewhere, look into the dark of the tunnel and then suddenly find a new station, new view, a new opportunity. They can recede into the haste of the metropolis and pretend to themselves that in a moment they'll alight, make their way above and that a mountain of important matters await their turn.

The metro has a great power of casting spells. That is why at the fall of evening when porters are closing the gates to the stairs, nearby, at its warm breath there are those who warm, those who are never in a haste anywhere at all.

Stadium

From a bird's eye view, the stadium is one of the most characteristic points written into the fabric of the city. Most, through its enormity. Huge, oval or round buildings burst the compact alignment of streets, lanes, squares and courtyards, overgrowing the meeting places of the everyday that surrounds them, an enormous imprint that reminds that days of set ritual are near.

During the week stadia are empty. As if haunting with their empty seats, while the carefully groomed grass pitch appears as a whimsy of maniacal gardeners. In times of difficulty stadia can turn into markets, in times of darkness they can function as concentration camps. Though the times of competition always await – it is then and only then that they come alive.

In the course of a two-thousand-year history, Europe has been witness to two periods when such gigantic constructions have been built. The first is the golden age of the Roman Empire. All of the Mediterranean seaboard is dotted with the ruins of arenas whose walls are embellished with classical arches as in the Colosseum and nowadays serve principally to attract tourists. It is not known really what else is possible. Host cities attempt to fill them by organising various ceremonies and festivals. Most often theatre productions. Though attempts to reanimate the dramas of the Ancient World in the ruins of great arenas do not really prove to be a success. Medea does not befit a circus. Several actors, a handful of audience, even the fantasy of lights does not bring back the life of a stadium orphaned some millennia ago. Elephants, lions, gladiators are requisite. And thousands of audience. For arenas live the crowd. A crowd of celebration. Huge football stadia that are built now only come alive when they are filled by thousands of thousands of red-hot shouting lookers-on. Just for these few hours.

The contemporary era is a second period of building great arenas. Though the style and art of engineering have changed radically in the course of two thousand years – it is after all in the form, the means of organising urban space that the obvious relation of these constructions can be seen. Does the Colosseum and stadium in Amsterdam therefore arise from the same spirit? And if so, what is their relationship?

We could suspect that it is the spirit of secular civilisation. This could be indicated by for example, the forgotten means of organising the living space of stadia. The places of action – arena, track or playing field – are encircled by stands brimful of audience. Their eyes all merge to the central, most earthly point, closed in from all sides of the human mass. They look down, under their selves, there where the 'players', made little by distance, struggle with the last ounce of their strength. Themselves finding fulfilment in the sharing of triumph for that very second or bitter defeat with thousands of other like-minded. Mostly like the case in Rome, and so it is today. The same as historian Henri-Irénée Marrou, characterising the Greco-Roman civilisation – the prime driving force of this epoch was the search for good fortune; the horizon narrows to the dimensions of human life within its earthly boundaries, to life as it is being lived.

What a contrast to the spaces of the cathedral where the eyes of the faithful follow the direction of the alter and above, over heads towards the light beyond, the earthly walls that fall into the temple. The mind searches for the not of the earth and not the human. Moreover, deserving note is the fact that the time of building cathedrals and time of building stadia does not overlap. In the course of twenty centuries of Christendom in Europe almost no arenas have been built. And certainly not out of a lack of skills.

The matter is not though, so simple. Doubt can be cast at least by Byzantium culture as no other focused on religious life and at the same time, torn asunder by sporting passions whose memory has survived to this very day in tales of premier clubs, the Green and the Blue. The battles of their supporters no doubt did not at all differ from the conflicts of Manchester and Amsterdam supporters. Moreover, in Byzantium there is probably the prototypical relationship of sporting passions with that of politics. If the royal court loved the Greens, then the opposition the Blues. Out of the ferocious collision of factions there began one of the most dangerous revolutions of this town, the uprising named *Nika*.

And at the same time it was a culture where discussion on godly nature was treated in truth very seriously. After all, those supporters took a passionate part – theological conflicts often were played out on the streets, in times of altercation where those representing the 'wrong' views and advocates on the 'wrong' side had their skulls broken. The crowds of long-haired supporters were led often by bearded monks and the fury of one side and the other was braced in common by the respective beliefs of heaven and earth.

It would seem that in this context the stadium hooliganism was permeated by a deep spirituality. However, the historian of Byzantine civilisation, Cyril Mango, has another explanation for its spread: Although hooliganism does not have its own philosophy, no one denies that it is a symptom of urban decadence, a crisis of values and widespread boredom. The most important words being 'urban' and 'boredom'.

Stadiums are typically urban works of civilisation. In fact ones of a metropolis. It is necessary that on a daily basis a great deal many people live in confinement so that the arena could house them from time to time. It is also necessary that these people know the meaning of free time. That their life be not only filled by the toil of the land, workshop, money exchange and factory. That their time be divided between times of boredom and times of competitive games.

Stadia live only for the times of competition. On such a day they are a hive of feverish activity, brimming with explosive energy, voicing a collective shout of ecstasy and enthusiasm. On the remaining days, however, they are empty, frightening, sadly empty. Waiting in boredom. Their vastness of being is one of waiting for that one short day, when the crowds arrive.

Stadia are therefore a palpable testimony to the heart of a metropolis, the life of a crowd. Its very quintessence. Making manifest how man exists – the one not especially relevant to anyone, but who in fact is. Stadia endow rhythm with substance, dividing time into long periods of grey boredom and short periods of games, holidays and recreation. Periods in which existence is channelled, intensified, joining with the existence of others, alike and defined itself in contrast to others, not alike. For a moment exploding in a gazer of energy, only to wallow in dingy rooms of metropolis peripheries, along streets littered in rubbish, in the superfluous.

Only ancient Rome and modern times have been able to create huge cities, filled with superfluous people. People that are cared for, entertained and flattered – for we do not know how else they can be occupied. Gigantic, monstrous stadia built to vast dimensions are the great monuments to these people. City crowds. Their superfluous nature swept the Empire away. Their superfluous nature is disintegrating modern civilisation. Perhaps in two millennia the representatives of the next civilisation with more than a shiver of anxiety and wonderment shall pay a visit to the empty stadia in Wembley and Chorzów – just as today we look upon the ruins of arenas in Nicaea and Pula.

Street Haiku

The billboard is a great advertising poster that gains everyone's attention – who happens to drive past the city streets. At the same time an artistic expression. Naturally, as is usually the case with artistic expression, the overwhelming majority is rather a babble – and only from time to time is there a diamond. Just as billboards. Most often they are shallow, based on worn out metaphors.

Sometimes though, the meeting of billboard image and word is a revelation – like someone's piercing glance caught in passing – a real Walter Benjamin thunderbolt. When a synthesis of meanings close to a point where everything locks in a tie of meaning, a capstone linking a train of thought. In the literary world the closest form to this is perhaps Japanese *haiku*. As for instance in the poem *Ice tastes bitter/In the mouth of the sewer rat/Quenching his thirst*,[6] of Basho, some four centuries ago. A good billboard is though the child of our times, which means it is meant for gazing. Usually language offers only a context for the figure. But also in fact in the skilful play of the context there lies the power of the billboard's message. Alike comics, yet another medium of the contemporary.

The poster, to remind us of the disabled. Portraying against a solid background the broken sculpture of the Hellenistic Cupid. Just this. Signed as: 'A child is greatly hurt'. Rough at the edges. Though... The play of meaning is based on a specific reality of classical sculpture in our imagination. Specific for it always calls forth the image of perfection broken. Nike of Samothrace, Venus or Apollo almost always has a missing shoulder, nose or even head. And in fact thus seen, these sculptures are for us the zenith of art, in reality their symbol. Perhaps in fact through their lack of completeness, through the disabledness of stone they are, for us, a symbol of perfection. If Nike had a head, Venus of Milo a shoulder... Of course this would be peculiar.

People, however, are the opposite. Appear perfect only when everything is as it should be – limbs and head screwed on the right way. Impairment inevitably changes our viewpoint, would appear to degrade – woman without arms, man without legs or a child disabled and incomplete. Who for that matter would want to have anything to do with them?

In placing the broken cupid side by side with a child, the artist is responsible for linking these two scales of judgement in the flash of an eye. One along which worn by the cogs of time, art ascends across its course and man descends, falling, a cripple. This provides the opportunity for the broken cupid in our imagination to take the crippled child there, where the cupid is destined – as a work of art – to be. In the sphere, it should be said, of the sublime.

---

6   Makoto Ueda *Matsuo Basho. The Master Haiku Poet*. Kodansha Int. Ltd. 1982, p. 46

Naturally, no one who has to fight for survival, driving a motor car along congested roads, does not reflect on the intersections of billboard messages. Though perhaps the passing brush with spheres of the sublime and the broken – that reaches the doors of the aware – will change something in the nature of reaction, reflex that a crippled person evokes. Perhaps it can even more successfully change than tales, articles or lectures.

One of the main criticisms against all manner of advertising art and therefore also posters or billboards is its submission to the demons of consumption. What type of art is it – repeat critics – that serves to muddle people's minds. It serves to encourage the superfluous ritual of shopping, to empty their wallets, to bring more unnecessary items home, to search for a place for them. Finally, so as to earn more money than one needs to spend. Notwithstanding, the above mentioned cupid serves in fact a totally different purpose, though whichever way one views this, it nonetheless does so. Continuing this form of reasoning we can accept that it is in fact an art of sorts, but one that is low, pop, servile – and quite frankly – impoverished. In contrast to high art, which is an aim in itself.

This criticism and the somewhat disparaging tone that accompanies it are based though on the assumption that art if it wishes to be a true art, it should be ostentatiously unbiased. Moreover, in subjecting creative work to other designs than artistic ones, the former by definition degrade the latter. What then can be done with the commonly observed fact that industrial design aspires to the world of museums and vernissages?

Those who deploy *design* and *art déco* to the purgatory of mass culture, nonetheless make a choice that is not in the least obvious. One can therefore claim that it is pure art – an invention of modernity – that is a type of aberration. Or rather that pure art is an emanation of highly defined assumptions in respect to the world and man. Throughout millennia it has been otherwise. Irish luminaries that filled the pages of the book of Kells with Celtic ornamentation did not serve art, but served God. Ditto the creators of Byzantine mosaics.

The creators of advertisements serve the idols of consumption. Idols befitting our time. Art though, if it does appear at times in advertisements, grows beyond that context, becomes autonomic. Then it is pure, the purest. A testimony to our age, when only ruins are left of supermarkets, to which one goes with a tour guide. A testimony such as mosaics and frescoes or Psalters brimming with illumination, reposing in museum showcases. And so read today as haiku is – after all, fulfilling the humble role of the initial verse of great, long forgotten epic poems.

Titanic

Once, in a totally different age, the Titanic sank. To be precise, the fatal collision with the iceberg took place on the night of April 14 1912. In the course of two and a half hours this symbol of English nautical might sank into oblivion and to this very day rests some four and a half thousand metres under sea. For those of us who know the events of the 20th century – full of catastrophes – in an age for us where almost every evening the 'magic eye' presents sinking towns, blazing villages and remains of aeroplanes strewn across this or other hillside, it is impossible to imagine the extent that the Titanic's misfortune caused. One thousand six-hundred people drowned, seven-hundred survived. Many or few? In the Great War, thirteen million perished. In the Second – fifty million. Many or few?

Historians at times comment that the 20th century and its belief in human reason ended in the trenches of Marne, Verdun and the Dukla Pass – thus continued up to 1914. In fact though, the turning point was the Titanic tragedy. This was the first sign that spelt out that positive faith rests in the positive might of human reason, to put it mildly, on frail foundations. This ship had no right to sink! A double hull. Five chambers that could be potentially isolated. An excellent – for those times – radio apparatus. A hundred thousand bid the Titanic farewell when on April 10 it farewelled the slipway in Southampton for its first journey....

And this in fact is important. Let us imagine what it would have meant at that time to gather a hundred thousand people. The ship was a symbol. A political symbol but also a symbol of human power over nature, over the elements, over fate itself. It was a symbol of a great myth, a bracket for the imagination of Europeans for at least fifty years. And great arrogance, in the Greek sense of the word *hybrys*. The attempt to escape beyond the assigned nature of man. The first ship with a swimming pool on deck. And seven bath houses. And orchestra. Taller than skyscrapers. For such arrogance retribution is inevitable.

For several thousand people the Titanic's sinking was simply a matter of human misfortune that struck them or their kin. Though for millions it became a sign. A forecast. A foretelling that the elements broke free, or perhaps worse, were never under control. Later simply the choking fumes of mustard gas at Ypres.

The press at that time sensed the strength of the myth that was born. When survivors reached New York, the New York Times renovated several rooms, installing (at that time!) totally new telephone lines so as to collect accounts of this tragedy. Then writers took to the Titanic. For example Erik Fosnes Hansen, who made the musicians of the deck orchestra the central point of his story. The orchestra as some of the survivors recounted – to the very last – played well known melodies, in the end only to sink into the icy water. Again cameo – sign, cameo – symbol. If someone had wished to invent a metaphor for *fin de siecle* they could have not found any better. And the Titanic orchestra par excellence has remained such a metaphor.

The 20th century *fin de siecle* was different. One of its traits is, as Baudrillard claims, a precession of *simulacra*. A curious word – *simulacrum*. *Simulacra* refer to *simulacra*. A product of the world in which contact with natural reality has been replaced by the invasion of an invented truth, one processed by an awareness filled entirely by symbols. One example of simulacrum is James Cameron's *Titanic*.

When at the start of the 20th century the Titanic tragedy became a symbolic fact, a metaphor at the close of a particular epoch, the meaning of this metaphor directed us to reality. Its referral point was the real catastrophe of a real ship. This catastrophe occurred in the real context of a particular social and political system. A foretelling of real civilisation catastrophes – wars, revolutions and 'revolts of the masses'. People across all the capitals of Europe were anxiously recounting the story of the orchestra to one another and the orchestra playing slowly, slipping into the waves, in a way sensed their fate. Thanks to this metaphor they attempted to give their foreboding a name.

The film about the Titanic did not fulfil such a role. It did not refer us to our real premonitions – though these perhaps, just as then, did not forecast anything particularly pleasant. This though was not the most important. Cameron's film in fact sent us to the legend of the Titanic. Sent us to the atmosphere of *fin de siecle* – playing with our senses in recreating the atmosphere whose metaphor – concentrating like a lens catastrophic premonition – was the tragedy of the Titanic.

This film – a *simulacrum* – created the materialised experience of our grandparents as the subject of the image. Lacan relates such a situation by saying it is not so much the object of their attention but rather their gaze that becomes the object of our gazes. Though this could put in another way – we have too many a memory to perceive what has just appeared. We could have felt that something dangerous lurks in the real future but for our gaze, reality has long since lost its flavour. *Simulacra* have covered it over. 'Once upon a time in a certain land that was called England, an enormous ocean liner was built...'.

Huge sums served to recreate this gaze. Cameron hired a Russian submarine to inspect the wreck, sent robots armed with cameras to its interior, built a gigantic swimming pool in Mexico where he reconstructed a model almost to scale of the ship. In the model, lined just like the original with teak, brass details and crystal chandeliers, even a reconstructed Marconi radio. Artists wandered, their faces making contemporary this uncontemporary tale. And only the Titanic Historical Society protested against these camera-armed robots setting about the ship's wreck. For this wreck was still a real cemetery. One not allowed to be desecrated in the name of the most successful games. Their voice though was a very quiet one.

Why then in fact have we assigned huge sums to raise a *simulacrum* from the dead? What purpose did this effort serve? This huge orchestration of technology and organisation and all its possibilities? Entertainment? What is so riveting in a repetition of living life, one consumed long ago by moths? Perhaps nostalgia was an explanation? And envy? Perhaps we recreated life as it was a hundred years ago so as to for at least a moment, feel what it was like when reality was basically true and its events were in fact its metaphor? Out of envy for then – at that time – something was real for people, to be taken seriously? So this was nostalgia for the age of naivety?

A nostalgic game of *simulacrum* in its emotions a hundred years ago had a lightness, until jumbo jets directed by suicide servants of Al Kaida crashed into the WTC Towers. One though unlikely, for often repeated image of planes striking into the building, created by the 21st century – sent it to the scrapheap. The falling popularity of subsequent television showings of the *Titanic* confirm that our view no longer searches in that direction. We have our own metaphor – there only remains what it in fact it portrays.

Let us love pop culture

Love pop culture! And if you cannot, at least give it a good once over. It is not therefore, unlike Hanna Arendt's view, a worthless process of goo from destroyed works of 'great' art. It is self-sufficient, a pulsating, alive contemporary, reality at the turn of the 21st century of those creating this world. More, mass culture reaches for spheres in essence not easily accessible for elite culture, reaches beyond its self-awareness. Therefore, if the culture of elites is one of self-consciousness, then mass culture can be called a culture of self-unconsciousness.

The disintegration of traditional society's myths was outlined, sometimes bemoaned, by a whole range of thinkers from Eliade and Kołakowski to the post-structuralists. In such works the following assertion is repeated: we have lost heaven and hell, guaranteed by faith and myth, a new infernum has taken outright hold, the hell of civilisation by the name of Void. In the meanwhile, while philosophers wring their hands over the ruins of traditional mythology, this Void is filling. Filling in leaps and bounds, suddenly, often in a grotesque manner. Filling for the appetite of Myth and Figure which is huge, one that shall embody the complex paths of meaning in human existence. The Void that has left the breakdown of traditional cultures – one that is not able to be taken by the culture of intellectual elites is filled by mass culture. Smelting the shards of various traditional systems, generating entirely new figures, it becomes the medium of signs and meaning perhaps best expressing what is known as the contemporary.

Naturally, in this place Hanna Arendt perhaps can return the accusation that mass culture fills this empty space – but with what?! A processed goo of works, temple of consumption, in essence acts of physiology. Nonetheless one could say that the assumption upon which this criticism is based – that consuming pop culture is a radical act and in essence differs from living Culture – is simply a mistaken one. This suggests as if together with the fall of traditional systems of culture, this space has in fact disappeared, which the former filled. That the Void in which mass culture is something totally different from that Space. Therefore one could say otherwise: the space has remained, its filling is changing and even, perhaps, its geometry.

Saying therefore that existence, human presence is still entangled and full of meanings, regardless of the fact that its character continues to change; no longer the times of King Oedipus, but the life of a roller skater in Warsaw or programmer from Shanghai. And signs and symbols are still needed, ones that embody these entangled paths of meaning. More, ones that are able to place them in the spheres of already existent meanings. This role in fact is played by pop culture. The importance of its particular accomplishments can vary. In spite of this not the garishness of colours or mixing of styles is the ultimate measure of their value but the depth, authenticity or coherence of meanings to which they refer. More later.

***

First, let us examine the mythical figure at the close of the 20th century, symbol of evil from the first Batman film, the Joker. The Joker in the pack of cards is one that can replace every other. The Joker does not live as self-sufficient – but takes on the guise the card it replaces. But the Joker cannot be this card. It is devoid of its own being, simply an empty form. It does not exist. As St Augustine teaches, evil is in fact a lack – a non-being. Therefore the Joker is evil, accounting for itself through a provocation of what exists, through a negation of a sense of what does exist. Itself threatened by Non-existence, the Joker exists when destroying what does. Through stripping what is their most important attribute – existence. Allowing it to reverse the sense of opposition, in being and non-being.

The Joker is an empty form. The false can fill the empty. Around the cinematic Joker there are many objects that are the main form. Turning meanings is possible when all becomes empty, when it is possible to destroy contents. Cosmetics, lipstick and powder are also forms within which the real contents of the face hide. It is with their help that the Joker attacks the city. You have bought something that is to change appearance only but it also changes the essence, substance, blighting the face. The Joker shows that one cannot without impunity play games with form.

In this move the Joker is the harlequin. Evil in the mask of sarcasm has for a long time fascinated, perhaps because it most clearly manifests the absurdity of evil in the world. Being is a trap for people. But a trap in the mask of laughter. And the arbitrary nature of evil that the Joker enacts, his absurdity, rips open this laughing mask, revealing the hidden sarcastic laugh. And revealing the false, turning sense, it gains a moment of existence. Taking the words of Octavio Paz, in its own way it is just, positioning things in their rightful place, meaning to dust, poverty and nothingness. His 'humour' is an act of revenge. For in the end, one turned towards the Void, the Joker knows that only through provocation can he exist amongst people...

This figure that appears on the screen is comprehensible from the first moment. This comprehension is not intellectual, no one conducts complex deliberations, does not reach us through discourse. The Joker does not utter a word that is not related to action. No one comments on his deeds, does not attempt to place them in a wider context. And that wider context though exists!

The Joker initiates spheres of experienced life that are not uttered by a single word in the film. A part can be spoken but there is always something else. Why? For the symbol is always richer than its interpretation. And interpretation is always late in terms of the symbol's meaning.

This in fact is the source of pop culture's power. The creators of mass art cannot afford the slightest moment of interpretation – their audience despise boredom, have to have time really filled by 'what happens'. But those in the audience, contrary to what Hanna Arendt claims, are not in addition deprived of those spheres of experience to which interpretations often refer. Spheres in which there are sub-conscious ties, situations, events and figures of existence. Ones present in the experience of everyone, for they are somehow present in collective experience known also as collective unconsciousness. This audience simply does not wish to hear of them, for after all, they are spheres of living, not thinking!

***

Let us rest our focus on the opposition of meanings, consciously understood and told, and those experienced or present in the unconsciousness. This is the key. If it were not there, Hanna Arendt would be correct.

The concept that a symbol is more complex than its interpretation comes from Ricoeur. It appears in deliberations relating to the symbolism of evil, specifically to the meaning of the serpent – tempter in paradise. This is the story more or less: had Ewa herself decided to pick the deadly fruit, the entire responsibility for evil would have rested upon the human species. The myth would say accordingly: man is fully responsible, is in every sense the creator of events that meet him. But in heaven there was also the serpent. Ewa herself took the decision to pick the apple – and if not for it, who knows.... This is the trap that was her life. And Ewa entered it but it was not she who laid it. So much for Ricoeur's interpretation.

Thus the question is: how many people that have participated in this myth over the past four millennia have consciously undertaken its interpretation? How many have discussed the various means of understanding its meaning? Zealots in ancient Jerusalem? Elderly German women admiring a painting by Cranach? Puritan lumberjacks in America reading the Book of Genesis? Hermeneutic deliberations were not at all required. The symbol though, moved them to the very core! It brought truth, one they never formulated but one that accorded in some way with their experience of the world. With their deepest convictions of life's meaning. This expressed itself in the reception of truth and power that resided in this symbol. And there was no, and is no, mediation of words necessary.

A similar tale perhaps – it should be stressed perhaps but does not have to – is told in the symbols of mass culture. It so happens that the concentration, the gulf of meanings contained in it is beyond our ken. Though at the same time they do not leave time for reflection. After all, action continues, after all bat-man is already flying on his last battle... By the way, why a bat?

The consequence of operating beyond the sphere of the verbal, by referring to the unconscious, is that pop culture avoids being entangled in discourse. And such entanglement poses a threat to every elite culture. Attempting to unusually often offer a sign together with its interpretation. Attempting to close in the past (though this past was a year before) something that exists in the present. Often interpretation itself becomes a sign. And though the creator does not hurry, it loses attributes that a pure (tempting to say bare) symbol carries. One that speaks beyond words. Always more complex than interpretation, and interpretation is always late in relation to it. Recording the changes of meaning that shall be discussed after many years, if not centuries. That is why it is necessary to love pop culture. And if not to love, then examine it carefully. For it is now.

The question of chaos

The feeling that meeting chaos leaves within us is strange. Strange, difficult to grasp for it is made up of elements that are in mutual opposition. No doubt it contains a mix of fullness and of continual, unabated hunger. It is also associated with a light dizziness, queasiness. Perhaps what happens to each of us after alighting from a carousel is a good metaphor here. But in this feeling there is also a suggestion of despair. At the same time a sort of unhealthy, feverish sense of excitement. And finally, a listless constant, lack of will for effort of any kind.

This condition shall be our milestone, guide in reflection. In this way we shall save the mind from losing track, easily done, when drawn into chaos.

Why is it so that chaos leaves a sense of lack? For in one way it is a synonym for completion. 'At the beginning there was chaos'. Chaos, thus everything. It is only from this 'allness' – synonymous to nothingness – that God creates beings. Not only in our Judeo-Christian tradition. Eliade maintains that the motif of chaos – the dragon – that needs to be vanquished so as to establish order in the world – is a constant figure throughout mythology and culture.

The widespread occurrence of this motif of battle indicates that our human means of reasoning is not content with an over full, chaotic 'completeness'. We react to it physically: fits of queasiness and headaches. It is only the appearance of some structure, something that organises the movement of awareness, ensures a state of soothing for our spirit. And the creation of constructs here belongs to the demiurge, God or a protagonist that establishes the lie of the land of a given culture.

Evening – eyes glued to the box. Cable television guarantees in the course of several hours, ten films, six discussions on very important subjects, several means of revealing one's naked all – in some incidental but well known way – as well as three news programmes, showing live the events across the world. Every film tells a tale of people, their feelings, their ups and downs. In the space of two hours we are witness to the most important moments of their life. Crying, making love, they die and rise – we, along with them. Then others die and cry – but this is news from the front in some Bosnia or Afghanistan. Later a very attractive and elegant girl, confesses to the female newsreader that she wishes to sing together with her cocker spaniel, whereupon the spaniel appears on the screen and howls. Mr. P. has the image of an old woman's tearful face but no longer knows if it's from the film on the invasion of Martians, or indeed from the report of an invasion of people.

Mr. P. can feel this state: queasiness and a suggestion of desperation in the background. Why did he not go out, to the park, so as to be in the thick of trees?

Though, had he gone, he would have stopped no doubt at the kiosk and bought a paper. Or a woman's magazine for his wife. And open, leaf through it and again be replete with the confessions of someone who simply does not in fact really exist. Or coloured pictures of green peas in a dish that he shall never make and eruptions of volcanoes about which he knows nothing, as well as information on the decisions of politicians who he never had and never will have, any influence over.

The question that we are attempting to answer is: what is the nature of chaos that packs contemporary culture? What is the essence and genesis of the phenomenon that arises in this state of spirit while part of this culture: a mix of superficial excitement, queasiness and listlessness with a suggestion of desperation as background? Let us put aside the obvious temptation of explaining this condition through the phenomenon of overflow, plain excess. A fact that the reality we are companions to is brimful, in fact overfull – though true it does not constitute what for chaos is the most characteristic.

Chaos is an organism that is devoid of structure in which a wide variety of elements sit side by side, overlap in a way that removes their independent meaning. Chaos is dangerously close in proximity to the non-organism, to nothingness. Chaos destroys its own elements, which through being intermingled lose importance and the fabric of their existence, becoming make-believe beings. Chaos though is not a void. A void allows thought for a free, though difficult creation. Chaos strangles the thought of make-believe beings, not allowing them to initiate movement but at the same time, never leaves one replete.

This is tied to the nature of our thinking, our awareness, which wanders from phenomenon to phenomenon in constant movement, but not a movement that is accidental. Every distinct thought, image, figure that is born in the space of my consciousness, already points to a subsequent thought, to a figure that complements it, to a road further, along which the spirit shall wander. This is its life. Without this the spirit begins to die. The structure that organises this wandering, usually remains hidden. But it is there. There like the ground underfoot. If it's not, dizziness appears, a lack mingled with overflow and despair.

Such an elusive structure hides in every thought, in every awareness. In fact in every reality that is a whole. Governed by a particular system, a particular unity of assumptions or intentions that can be felt in the gamut of appearances, products phenomena. And our thoughts meeting these phenomena, accompanying them in fact behave like a hand in the dark attempting to recognise some object.

Further contact, movement, fragments caught in thought, we reconstruct the hidden shape and the further we search, the more we sense the existence of what we make contact with. If, however, the senses that reach us do not form into an integrated whole, if one experience contradicts another, anxiety and depression arise. In as much as the extent of these contradicting and unrelated feelings grow, in as much they confront our thinking, it surrenders and wallows in nothingness with the feeling that the ground underfoot is slipping. Feeling, our *vademecum*.

***

It is said that the Gothic is a school of thought transferred into dimension. The Gothic world is based on the desire of Abbot Suger and the concepts of St Thomas Aquinas. Regardless whether we examine the buttresses of the Notre Dame Cathedral or the brick arches of crusaders' churches and the vaulting of the Grand Master's Palace in Malbork, we shall find everywhere a unified theme, a common plan. A hierarchy of matter ascending upwards and light falling downwards – upwards and downwards – a means of organizing the world in a powerful and transparent way. It is the work of a thousand people who worked over hundreds of years. A common plan in place, for them, a common initiative that we discover, one we are able to identify with for a while.

Was this simply the framework of Abbot Suger's mind or a certain model of the world that embraces everything and everyone? And maybe in the Abbot's thinking only this plan appeared, another embodiment finding itself in *The Summa Theologica* of St Thomas Aquinas? Undoubtedly it was a certain unified philosophy, one spirit whose effects are scattered across the seas from England's Thames to the East European River Bug. Man, wandering through the Europe of that time, encountered either works of nature or one integrated by a common spirit.

And what does man encounter, wandering through this dimension today? The works of nature are blanketed over by constructions out of plastic, concrete and steel competing for attention with billboards, enormous motorway road signs, information on what and who makes what, as well as sound-reduction constructs, high voltage lines, coloured rubbish tips, supermarkets in neon, lamps on posts and posts per se and things that in general are very difficult to imagine. Naturally, somewhere there is also a dimension for the Gothic, Renaissance and Baroque of old.

Even this gamut of approaches, however, is not the source of dizziness or sense of over-fullness tied to a hunger for more and despair. These feelings do not hide (at least not foremost) in the company of real objects that make up the real dimensions of the world in which we make our way. We are not focused on them but on the real world in fact of matters that are seeming: the stream of images, thought and sounds that reach us from the net, from radio when we are travelling and television, when sitting at home, from newspapers and advertising posters, books and magazines, interviews, discussions and intimate confessions.

When we live with material objects, even with material products of culture, we are forced into the effort of identifying meanings hidden in them, intentions behind their graspable form. Further, we need to often build meaning ourselves, organise the world according to a particular myth that each of us carry within. Into the existence of the reality that we have to place our own work. The numbing power of this chaos, one that reaches us from screens, speakers and even written narratives, is based on our liberation from the effort of identifying and creating our world. We receive various worlds that are already packaged, images laid out in some sort of whole, meaning we can think the thoughts of others. Passivity, lethargy – this in fact attracts us.

We pay though with the feeling that unnoticed, the ground underfoot is slipping. Because every one of these images, streams, magnets of thought, belong to another world. Each in their own spirit, own assumptions, sensibilities. Each woven to another form. Though each meet and mix in our within: the affirmations of a chanteuse for a love for animals, a pilot's memoirs brimmed with patriotism. The parody of adventures in the cult series Dzyndzy Lyndzy (or perhaps Ryndzy Lyndzy) and stock market analysis with Greenspan, Obama and Maclaren wedged in. Here awakes in Mr. P. a longing for the patriotic melody *First Brigade*, while here an appetite for Chinese cuisine – though any moment some thought of a mass grave will disgust me only to be laid over with someone's erotic fantasies... And the spirit all the more acts as if it was dealing with something completely amorphous, devoid of form and essence. And in it awakes dizziness, queasiness...

And increasingly therefore we are part of a processed world, the emanation of the minds of tens and hundreds of people meeting incidentally in common – journalists, cameramen, radio reporters, script writers, columnists, writers, fashion designers, architects, scholars, wardrobe assistants, directors, actors and singers. In addition – in contrast to the builders of cathedrals, each of the above fights for their inimitable position. For their products of intellect to be unique, standing out in a completely unrepeatable style and spirit. Such is the world of media, world of the contemporary media culture that with enormous strength it comes to possess our attention, our thoughts, our spirit.

***

The sense of chaos arises out of a mixing. The fact that every mind that creates has its own unique essence and by nature imposes its own vision of the world . When though they at the same time impose their vision of the world and their unique essence, when at the same they wander upwards and downwards, in red and black, wallow in the undefined and the shout, then one begins to feel queasy, feel despair. And this is not simply a question of choice that everybody needs to make. The intensity and thick of these various visions, feelings, sensitivities, their mutual proximity in time and space, on screens, newspapers, radio, walls of houses, means that there is no place for choice. Only a mindless race for them, with the sense of an ever greater distance from the essence of things.

Mr. P. thinks we are the victims of our own all pervasive might. Might, where almost every person that wishes can instil others with their vision of the world, thoughts, imaginings – simply their own person. From the time of Gutenberg, technology has come to serve the traffic of thought and constantly creates anew methods by which it is increasingly easier, increasingly quicker to cast out your interior worlds. Suffice to throw out your elbows and fit between the dreams of those who devour fantasy meals, the imaginings of long past battle-weary combatants. We have constructed and continue to construct a world built of neighbouring imaginings that overlap tens and tens of thousands of people in whom dwell countless totally different, and in no way mutually comparable, spiritual assignments.

The point of the matter, thinks Mr. P., is not that we be careful that the fantasies of Abbot Suger and St. Thomas Aquinas were in any way privileged in relation to those of the average journalist now, merchant or poet. I am not part, he claims, of any anti-modernist tradition. Fantasies are fantasies – period. Some worlds can be more beautiful, others less so – some a programme that embraces all, others remind of a small photograph – a pastel landscape hanging on a wall. But each is unique, one of its kind and in fact totally self sufficient. If my mind begins to live in accord with any of such programmes, then the birth of another means a disintegration within, disintegration of the previous, disintegration of a certain existential structure that I have built in the footsteps of my past guide and the need to build a new construct. Often, in fact, in conflict with the previous in its assumptions.

The problem though lies in the fact that in order to remain part of life, take part, be in time, Mr. P. like every other, feels compelled to constantly ingest the mutually entangled imaginings coming from completely different minds and worlds, from completely different programmes of reality, ones affecting at the same time various levels of sensitivity. Perhaps he is the more aware of this, for he has long lived in the desert. Today though, the fallout of all this appears in his mind as an eclectic, incoherent state, one that at the beginning we described as feverish and queasy, with a suggestion of despair as backdrop.

The cat and spider – where lieth force?

In the postmodern era, strength has had to don a mask. Had to begin to pretend that it has nothing to do with strength. Resorting to strategies that hide its true and lawful nature – in the direction of domination. Therefore – paradoxically – in a world ruled by rivalry and continual battle over taking up a position, openly striving for domination is condemned and branded as stigma. The way out from this paradox is illusion – strategies that mask the striving for domination.

The two most often applied are seduction and moral blackmail. Seduction, based on the enthralling power of pulsating beauty, allows to dominate without resorting to force. Moral blackmail though, appearing always on behalf of the victim, uses force, which pretends a lack of will to dominate. The ambassadors for such strategies wage a quiet war with one another, one that at times breaks out in a sudden noise. Paradoxically though, these strategies are mutually dependent – one justifies the other and both thrive on weakening the position of reason.

From the point of view of investigators of domination, in the late modernity, force not so much as donned a mask, as rather changed it. In their view, in modern times power has served the mask of rationality. Tearing this mask off has forced it to search for other guises. Because it has transpired that the rhetoric of outraged seekers of domination gave them a great power, force in a natural way reached for outrage as a new mask hiding violence. Discourse revealing domination became the mask of domination.

This paradoxical effect was possible, for the aim of those who sought to reveal is never a neutral disclosure – that this or the other is a mask for power. In the footsteps of disclosure follows moral judgement, one that is to destroy the propensity itself for domination, regardless of what happened to hide under the mask. The revealers usually are bursting with holy outrage and the manner in which they speak of power stripped naked reminds one of standing the accused before a pillory. This radical tone of accusation becomes, unnoticed, a form of violence. Thus as observed Nietzsche: "to require of strength that it should not express itself as strength, that it should not be a wish to overpower, a wish to overthrow, a wish to become master, a thirst for enemies and antagonisms and triumphs, is just as absurd as to require of weakness that it should express itself as strength(2003:25)".[7]

Strength baited and followed everywhere up to now where it could simply exist in accord with its own nature, intuitively sensed the violence present in the commandments of those who moralise. In this way it found a new form into

7   Friedrich Nietsche, *The Genealogy Of Morals*, Dover Publications 2003.

which it could slip. And is still present in our world. Why can't it be eliminated? For contrary to views holding man's angelic nature, in the workings of the community it is conflict and domination that have played a very important organisational role.

Human motives, which always forced to a lesser or greater open application of strength – enforcing defined means of functioning, influencing actions and feelings of others, strengthening the position of the former in various types of hierarchies or finally, improving a sense of happiness – and as it turns out, are in fact tied to the common good. That is why, excluded from one realm and disclosed, the game of domination returns to other areas in new guises.

***

The abandonment of rationality and acceptance of the position of outrage though – even if both one and the other mask the drive for domination – draws serious consequences. In the area of thinking determined by outrage there is no place for objectivity. If the instruments of rational analysis are seen to be the tools of violence, and the intention itself of understanding is treated as a sign of a thirst for authority, it is very difficult to conduct a conflict. Paradoxically therefore, outrage forces one to take the position *before* understanding the core of the antagonism.

Then intellectual helplessness, however, is in the company of arbitrariness and ungiving of judgements. Neither is it possible that the argument of one side take the upper hand. In such a context the other side's injury immediately appears. This contradiction also propels towards placing conflict immediately in the moral sphere. If one right takes the upper hand from the start and defines itself as the right of loss injury, then its domination shall be protected from the act of condemnation. Leading to a situation in which all rights, so as to survive, have to take on the mask of lost innocence...

How did this variegated substance arise? It is possible to find an explanation in the suggestion relating to the emotional character of our epoch. Thus in the modern world, expectation in relation to the future begin to increasingly become distant from all gathered by collective experience. Traditional cultures expect that future events shall be a repetition of times aplenty in the past. Again, as every year, there will be harvests, celebrations of the crop, times of plenitude. These types of expectations are tied to the cyclical concept of time. All repeats, all has to return in the same form. But when time flows along a straight line, from a defined beginning to an expected end, the line of thinking changes. The expected events are now never the same as those in the past. Expectations distance themselves from experience. In this approach there is a deep ambivalence encoded in relation to the world-as-it-is. So as to expect something else, man has to admit that this world is evil. Man has the right to judge it and set out in search of something that is not there.

But on what fundament does the right to judge the world rest? This fundament is injustice. The lament echoing in the Book of Prophets is already a forecast of one who is the victim of a heartless world. There is, however, a great difference between the cry of Job and the rebellion of modern man. The former is simply in despair. Therefore the latter's refusal to condone the evil of past experience signifies the right to a future redress. Upon receiving, Christian heritage in hand and capacity for hope, in modernity he takes the subject out of eternity into the future, changing hope into expectation.

This is a very important move. Changing itself into expectation, hope inevitably nears the gateway of disappointment. Man casts aside a spiritual situation characteristic for the Middle Ages and when placed into the transcendental, hope protected man from the prospect of the world's poverty. Approaching a position where hope appears to be a matter of promise. A continually unfulfilled promise. Hope therefore begins to be lined with impatience.

Such an expectation lined with impatience is not immune to the passing of time. After a while irritation appears that fulfilment is still not complete. 'Still not' – asks expectation. Such a stance is known as Gnostic and in this sense, as Voegelin writes, all of modern times are such. In addition, regardless, no matter how much is accomplished, disappointment appears all the same. For dreams are always more beautiful than reality. The Church of the Middle Ages understood this and fought Gnostic heresies with fire, sword and the word. It did not allow for hope – the keystone of faith – to change into expectation.

In modern times expectations have replaced hopes. Found another means though, to protect themselves from disappointment. No matter how bad the experience, it was justified through future fulfilment. Justified by the modern idea of progress. Written by Hegel into the iron laws of dialectics, it allowed one to interpret the present as a rather unimportant foretaste of the future.

The dialectic though did not survive. The hypothetical necessity of the laws of history disintegrated into ashes when the cry of those dying on return tore away the present from the future. It is not possible to propose a vision when a cry like a knife stabs the brain. It is at this moment that the well known metaphor of Walter Benjamin becomes relevant. The angel of history turns his back on future, happy generations. Gazes at those wronged. Cannot help. Cannot give their death a meaning. The totality of the inability to find a rational explanation for the gigantic crimes of the 20th century – most of all the Shoah – has deeply changed our thinking.

We have read: in the void that was born after Promethean hope vanished, the Shoah presented itself in all its nakedness and with its burden gave rise to a totally new order, a new means of receiving that became the axis and milestone. It is in fact this change that is a key for the system in which the 'disclosure of reason' took place. Changes in expectations turned disappointment and the dissemination of the discourse of the wronged. The phenomenon of strength, striving for domination, had to start looking for a new mask.

The trauma of crimes in the 20th century has had one more consequence. We can no longer rest upon the future such as the modern world in the age of its innocence. The past, a wellspring of meanings for truly traditional societies, has long since already seen disenchantment. Time's horizon therefore, has been filled by the inflated bubble of the present. And in it, two absolute orders struggle for primacy. Both reach for eternal rules. Whilst the discourse of injustice and law accuses, the discourse of beauty and taste, seduces. Or makes a mockery.

Everyone one of these orders organises the world in a way that does not allow to relativise. According to moralists the formula 'I suffer, therefore I am' replaced *cogito*. This justifies therefore new demands. Today now even repressed fragments of the body demand social acceptation. For those on the other hand, who wish to defend themselves from moral blackmail, there remains only the aesthetic judgement. Paradoxically, beauty in the modern world does not have to justify itself. Everything else is forced to rationalise its existence, whilst beauty not. Is it so because Kant moved this from the sphere of the reason of discourse, or perhaps because people have an innate universal sense that it recognises? One way or another, the desire for beauty is akin to a spell that unnoticed, though commonly, renders our senses helpless. This power allows it to sarcastically – and often cruelly – laugh at moralisers in their face.

***

From his childhood Mr P. remembers the following scene. In a bright, almost empty room a small cat is crawling with a rather clumsy grace towards a sunny large spot, which a black large spider is trying to cross in a hurry. The spider stops for a moment, most likely notices the cat approaching, swaying in hesitation, eyes of blue staring at the black shape. Heart in the throat – a flight of fright. What will happen when the black shape – in waiting with its poisonous antennae – makes contact with the cat, totally unawares. Out of the blue a lightening pounce. Almost unnoticed a flurry.... In the sunny large spot stands a small furry cat, and from his mouth there protrude only three or four sadly bent spider legs. And the enormous, careful eyes searchingly check the remainder of the room.

Mr. P. remembered the wave of relief that he felt at the time. The furry ball did not come to any harm. Only after many years did the real meaning of this scene occur. The cat killed the spider. Across the floor then, two predators met – but the more effective, more murderous, turned out to be the beautiful. Beauty, however, which we experience as familiar, protected it from being condemned. The spider, walking repulsion, was condemned to loathing. Regardless that his only fault was to crawl out of the dark corner, in which he no doubt was safe. Mr. P. was blind to the spider's injustice. Blinded by beauty.

These two orders – moral and aesthetic – give the impression they mutually exclude. Paradoxically, however, the strength exercised by priests of taste is tied strictly with how demonstrations of injustice dominate. What is the basis of this relationship?

The strength of aesthetic criteria signifies a change from a conflict of who was right, encroaching onto the field of rationality into a game of desire and gluttony. Domination is not based on the strength of rational argument but on the possibility of having available what is desired. It is not necessary to force anyone to do anything – suffice to seduce such that they desire. Subjugation though is complete only when the object of desire remains unobtainable. The power of beauty is thus all the more embedded the less there are legal means of reaching for it.

And here there appears an unexpected gain, which the priests of taste derive from a categorical condemnation of strength announced by representatives of those wronged. When the gesture itself of reaching for the desired is condemned by moralists there occurs a disturbance of balance between those desiring and the object of desire. The side that is beautiful, desired and unobtainable gains an enormous advantage. The lights trained, ostentatiously visible, feeding on the gazes fixed on it, derive strength and existence. The society of the spectacle. The one who desires, however, caught in the vice of moral outrage, unnoticed becomes an easy target of domination.

Every exhibition, unfolding ritual of image that renders the Gaze helpless – is the embodiment of this intellectual figure. And the one that personifies ritual, places itself in the centre of our field of imagination. Our culture has as if forgotten that once it was said: 'thou shalt not lead to temptation'.

***

It was only recently that it seemed it shall last another 100 years. But no, the game of priests of taste versus the prophets of seeking justice will not be resolved, we do not know their next moves. As in the sinking of the Titanic, which reminded 19th century society of something important tied to the relationship between man and nature, so too the violent events at the turn of the century, starting with the World Trade Centre has made us realise that even in the very centre of the civilisation of the late modernity, naked violence is still present in relations between people. In the sensibilities of our civilisation something irreversible has changed again. And in the context of this change, the conflict between 'seducers' and the 'outraged' begins to appear as *passé*. Again the need for rational understanding seeks to return.

We search for the lost measure that allows to think more clearly on matters that arise. A measure that came to characterise the Greek concept of Nemesis as wrote Simone Weil in 1939-1940: 'The Occident, however, has lost it, and no longer even has a word to express it in any of its languages: conceptions of limit, measure, equilibrium, which ought to determine the conduct of life are, in the West, restricted to a servile function in the vocabulary of technics'.[8]

There is no return to an act of innocent though cruel rationality – more or less so accorded to the Enlightenment. The present demands a philosophy that allows for the heritage of 20th century catastrophes. Again we reach for sources and search for understanding, one that in contrast to that of the Odyssey can be found, as Simone Weil proposed, in the Iliad. If in the Odyssey, as critics of the modern world claim, there arises an instrumental and objectified means of thinking, the Iliad can be read, as a record of disastrous human experience, one of a war-that-always-is. Thus a conscious placement, side by side of triumph as humiliation and subjugation. It is only from this experience that a search can arise for a sense of measure and consequently, a philosophy where the tools of intellect are not an ambush. A philosophy that does not allow a predator agent to snatch reality, but rather one that develops self-imposed ties so as to be as one with the world.

---

8   'The Illiad, or the Poem of Force, p.14 – reprinted in *The Chicago Review*, 18:2 (1965), translated by Mary Macarthy and revised by Dwight Macdonald.

Modernity in Question
Studies in Philosophy, Sociology and History of Ideas

Edited by Małgorzata Kowalska

www.peterlang.de